Happy
Orchard cooking
Beth!

Best wishes,
Stuart

The Orchard Cook

The Orchard Cook

RECIPES FROM TREE TO TABLE

STUART OVENDEN

CLEARVIEW

CLEARVIEW

First published in the UK in 2018
by Clearview Books
22 Clarendon Gardens,
London W9 1AZ

Compilation © 2018
Clearview Books, London
Text & images © 2018
Stuart Ovenden

ISBN 978-1908337-467

www.clearviewbooks.com

Editor: **Suzannah Dick**
Photography & styling:
Stuart Ovenden
Design: **Lucy Gowans**
Production: **Simonne Waud**

Printed in Europe
Colour reproduction by
XY Digital, London.

CLEARVIEW

Member of
MGIP

Contents

A cook in the orchard

Some of my earliest memories are of the orchard in the village. The footpath through to my old junior school takes you briefly through a long, valleyed wood, then past dark hedges of lush rhododendrons that lie along the south-western edge of the Manor. As you near the church and cemetery, the path quickly strikes a straight, diagonal line through the middle of the orchard, a crab apple tree planted at each end.

I often wondered why the crab apples were there; to me they seemed to offer no apparent merit to the casual scrumper, nor (and more importantly) the owner of the orchard. I know now why crab apples are planted in commercial orchards; they have a long flowering period in spring and are terrific pollination partners for cultivated apples - the delicate balance of an orchard is an important one. The walk to school took us through trees festooned with blossom in spring, heavy crops of fruit hanging off branches in late summer and the muggy ferment of the last days of autumn, air thick with dust and vinegar. I often think of an orchard as an almost self-contained environment; there's something appealing about the vivid polarization of the seasons that it offers up each year.

As a resource for food and drink, the orchard brings with it a wide spectrum of opportunities. It's not just about the fruit – I've found that you can use pretty much everything. Blossom, leaves, branches; one can even grind the kernels from the stones of a certain kind of cherry to make Mahleb, a spice used in recipes from Greece through to the Middle East. Orchard cooking needn't be just about apple pies and tarte tatins, although I have a great fondness for both and have included recipes for them in this book. The crisp freshness of an apple works perfectly with shellfish such as oysters and scallops, while plums and cherries have a natural affinity with game. Quince on the other hand, pairs well with the flavours of North Africa – Morocco in particular.

This book is a collection of recipes based around a year spent in a mixed fruit orchard, and while the seasonal emphasis naturally leans toward the autumn months, it's important to view orchard cooking as a year-round pursuit. There are recipes for spring, summer and winter included in the chapters; it feels only natural to want to spend as much time as possible in these beautiful, complex spaces.

The Orchard year

Spring draws us into the year enthusiastically. The bud burst of cherry blossom is sudden; an exuberant display of life that is striking, colourful but also precariously fragile. Delicate flowers sway on the tips of branches; a late frost or sudden gust of wind can be ruthless. It's a time of uncertainty, but also of great hope for the coming year. There are small harvests to be had – young cherry leaves can be pickled, while a discrete handful of cherry blossoms can be used to decorate a cake, or made into delicate, tea-like infusions.

Summer is green and lush. The arrival of the first ripe cherry marks a moment of unbridled joy for both us and the local indigenous wildlife. The birds have a keen eye and will make it away with a tree-full of cherries quicker than you can say clafoutis – netting is essential. While the cherry battle rages, pears, apples, quinces, plums and medlars are approaching readiness. Early apples such as Discovery and Worcester Pearmain are ready to be picked from mid-to-late August, both of which boast summery notes of strawberry.

Autumn is the busiest time of the year, as one would expect. From the first plums, through to the last of the apples, pears and quinces, the kitchen is always at the centre of proceedings. I'm poaching, pickling, baking, roasting – trying to make the most of a brief window of opportunity. A weekend set aside for cider making represents the high point of the season; the air at home is ripe with the sharp tang of apple juice fermenting in barrels and demi-johns. As autumn nears its close, any surplus fruit is prepared for storage to extend the harvest through the lean winter months.

The onset of winter doesn't strike a line underneath the orchard year. There are trees to prune – all cuttings are kept, chipped and used for hot and cold smoking. It's a time to take stock but also to enjoy the rewards that a year of hard work brings. A hip-flask of damson gin shared with friends on a chilly winter walk, a slice membrillo with a wedge of good cheese, or a few pickled cherries with cold meats at Christmas. If stored correctly apples, pears and quinces can keep all the way through to late winter.

Starting an orchard

It would be wrong to think that one needs an expanse of fruit trees, spilling across vast acres of land to be able to claim possession of what is officially termed, 'an orchard'. You need five, to be exact. This small number of trees is often referred to as a 'kitchen orchard', but it's an orchard nonetheless and a rather exciting prospect.

Position and weather

Fruit trees favour a south or south-west facing position, preferably on a slight slope to give good drainage and avoid over-wet roots. It can be tricky finding the optimum spot; if an orchard is too exposed it can be susceptible to the weather. On the flip side, if your orchard is enclosed by tall, pre-existing trees, it might not get the sunlight it needs to grow healthily, disease-free and produce-good fruit. Plant sympathetically to your climate; if you are prone to late frosts in spring, planting late-flowering or frost-resistant varieties is a shrewd move.

Varieties

Your choice of varieties is an important one that should be ultimately led by what you see yourself doing in the kitchen with the fruit further down the line. Remember that this is a long-game; depending on the initial size of tree and rootstock, it might be couple of years until you get a small crop, and longer still until you've got a glut on your hands. Think about when you want to eat and use your fruit; early-cropping apples are great to kick off the season but they won't keep, whereas late-season varieties are better for storing through the winter months. Pollination grouping is also something to consider when choosing trees. For example, some varieties of plum are self-fertile. For the most part however they flower at staggered intervals depending on variety, require cross-pollination, and need to be planted with this in mind. The Merryweather damson and Victoria plum bear blossom at the same time, so make for great orchard chums.

Rootstock

A rootstock is a pre-existing clump of roots, taken from a similar species of tree to which your chosen variety is joined by grafting or budding. By choosing a certain rootstock, one can predict growth rate and get an idea of the vigour and approximate end-height of a tree. An apple, pear, plum, cherry or medlar tree is stronger and healthier when grafted on a pre-determined root system, it also produces a true fruit. Most fruit trees reproduce through cross-pollination, which has no bearing on the flesh of the fruit itself, but the seed will be a hybrid; a genetic cross between the original tree and the variety that pollinated it. Quinces grow on their own rootstocks, usually either Quince A and Quince C – stocks which are also commonly used for pears. Rootstocks vary from vigorous to dwarfing, so choosing the right one is important. An apple grafted onto a vigorous M25 rootstock will produce a large tree with strong roots and need staking (supporting with a post) for the first few years. M27 however will produce a small tree that will need permanent staking – it's perfect for those with restricted space though. Fruit trees are sold as either bare-rooted or container-grown, the choice of which will determine when in the year to plant the tree.

Walled gardens

If open space is an issue, the branches of most fruit trees can gradually be trained horizontally along wires, while sitting against a wall or sturdy fence. This technique is known as espalier. The sight of an old espalier apple or pear in a Victorian walled garden is a fine one; trees trained against walls can also benefit from the heat retained in bricks after a hot day. Another way of maintaining an orchard in a confined space is to grow cordons. This involves manipulating the growth of the tree as a single stem, with fruit swelling on short branches that grow close to this central point. Espalier and cordon training are by no means the only way of manipulating tree growth in smaller plants, but they are a great starting point in terms of getting the most out of fruit trees in compact areas.

Pruning

It's general practice to prune apple, pear, quince and medlar trees while they are lying dormant over the winter months, between leaf-fall in late autumn and the arrival of blossom in spring. Plum and cherry trees differ in that they should only be pruned when in full growth (late spring to mid-summer) to prevent exposing them to diseases and fungal infections. Most apples and pears produce fruit on branches that are a minimum of two years old; pruning is essentially about retaining shape, removing diseased, broken branches and creating an uncongested branch network for fruit to be able to grow efficiently.

Thinning

Many fruit trees set more flowers than they actually need each spring and naturally drop some of their immature fruit in summer. This is known as the 'June drop', which can be rather alarming when you see the amount of fruit shed beneath a tree, but it pays to bear in mind that only one or two blossoms out of 20 are needed to produce a full crop on an apple tree. Further thinning after June is usually necessary to avoid overcrowded, clusters of fruit that are unable to reach their optimum size. I tend to remove all but two of the best-looking apples or pears in a group; it's a good time to get rid of any smaller, misshapen or diseased-looking fruit. Plum trees may also need thinning, although I find that this is less of an issue with quince and medlars.

Conversion tables

Oven temperatures

140°C	275°F	Mark I
150	300	2
170	325	3
180	350	4
190	375	5
200	400	6
220	425	7
230	450	8
240	475	9

Lengths

3mm	⅛ inch
5mm	¼ inch
Icm	½ inch
2cm	¾ inch
3cm	1¼ inch
4cm	1½ inch
5cm	2 inches
20cm	8 inches
23cm	9 inches
30cm	12 inches

Weights

7g	¼ oz
15g	½ oz
20g	¾ oz
30g	I oz
55g	2 oz
85g	3 oz
110g	4 oz
125g	4½ oz
140g	5 oz
170g	6 oz
200g	7 oz
225g	8 oz
255g	9 oz
285g	10 oz
310g	11 oz
340g	12 oz
370g	13 oz
400g	14 oz
450g	I lb
675g	1½ lb
900g	2 lb
1.35 kg	3 lb

Liquid measures

15ml	½ fl oz
28ml	I fl oz
55ml	2 fl oz
75ml	3 fl oz
150ml	5 fl oz (¼ pint)
190ml	6.6 fl oz (⅓ pint)
290ml	10 fl oz (½ pint)
570ml	20 fl oz (I pint)
I litre	35 fl oz (1¾ pints)

Apples

Apples

It's a bitterly cold January morning. The orchard looks threadbare; frost clings onto leafless branches, giving them an almost coral-like glow in the bright winter sun. The trunks of the trees are protected from wild animals by wire mesh, but a pile of fruit tree cuttings tucked into the copse are fair game — their bark has been stripped away gradually, scarce pickings gleaned from a succession of visits by deer under the cover of darkness. Meagre times for everyone it seems; it's hard to imagine that in about seven months' time the first of the early-season apples will be ready to pick.

Apples make up over three quarters of the fruit trees in the orchard. There's a broad spectrum, plenty of eating and cooking apples — most are heritage varieties but there are a few modern exceptions. They range from Warner's King, a huge eighteenth-century cooker, Kingston's Black, a bittersharp cider apple from Somerset, to Deacon's Millenium, a crimson, sweet eating apple that has vibrant magenta flesh when cut. Some of the stories behind the apple names are often as intriguing as the fruits themselves. One of my favourites is the Bloody Ploughman, which is reputedly named after a farm worker who, after being caught stealing apples, was chased through the orchard by a gamekeeper and shot. The stolen apples were thrown onto a compost heap — the trees that grew from the pips were named after the poor fellow that scrumped them. Like a macabre fairytale, probably with a varying degree of truthfulness, but engaging nonetheless.

There are over 7,500 varieties of apple grown worldwide. It's widely thought that all domesticated apples are ancestors of Malus sieversii, a wild apple that grows on the Tien Shan mountain range bordering China and Kazakhstan. While there is evidence to suggest that crab apples grew wild in England during Neolithic times, there doesn't seem to have been any attempt to cultivate the trees. It's more likely that the ball started rolling when Romans introduced sweeter, better flavoured apples and grafting techniques during their occupation, while the Normans brought a strong tradition of apple growing and cider making with them after the conquest of 1066. A seemingly unlikely champion of the apple cause was Henry VIII, who was passionate about fruit and established England's first fruit collection at a site in Teynham, a village close to the Isle of Sheppey in Kent.

Apples are wonderfully varied in flavour; I've tasted lemon, strawberry, pineapple — the old French variety Nonpareil even has a distinct pear drop taste. Cooking apples tend to be large in size and sharp — their acidity mellows with heat, time and most importantly, sugar. Plenty of eating apples cook well too, varieties such as Egremont russet hold their shape and are perfect for tarte tatins. These are fruits to be enjoyed; sometimes cooked, sometimes tossed through a salad, or sometimes eaten simply, straight off the tree on a warm autumn day.

Apfelkren is an apple and horseradish sauce traditionally served in Austria with roast beef, but it's just as good an accompaniment to pork. The horseradish kick works wonderfully when paired with the sharp sweetness of apple.

Roast pork loin with Apfelkren

Serves 4

For the roast pork:

1.2kg pork loin on the bone, skin on. This piece fed 4 people; it's easy to upscale though - just add 30 minutes extra cooking time for every 500g extra weight. If you can, ask the butcher to saw a groove across the ribs at the base of the joint; it makes it a lot easier to pull the meat away from the bone when carving.

a few garlic cloves and sprigs of rosemary

For the apple and horseradish sauce:

3 medium-sized Bramley apples

50g caster sugar

50g freshly grated horseradish

juice of 1 lemon

1 About an hour or so before cooking, take the pork out of the fridge. Crosshatch the skin with a Stanley knife, then rub with salt. Set to one side – the salt will draw moisture out of the skin (creating better crackling), while the time elapsed before cooking allows the pork to warm to room temperature (which is better for roasting). Now's the time to season the rest of the meat, make small incisions in the flesh and poke in a few garlic cloves and rosemary sprigs.

2 Preheat the oven to 240C(220C fan), Gas 9. Stand the meat on a roasting tray with the skin facing up and roast for 20 minutes. Turn the heat down to 190C(170C fan), Gas 5 and cook for a further hour, or until the core temperature has reached 68C when checked with a meat thermometer. Rest in a warm spot for 15 minutes before serving; don't cover – you'll spoil the crackling if you do.

3 Peel, core and roughly chop the apples. Tip into a saucepan with the sugar and a splash of water, then stir on a medium heat until for 10-15 minutes until they have broken down to a near-purée. Take off the heat, cool for 10 minutes then stir in the horseradish and lemon juice.

It isn't spring until ramson shoots have begun to appear along the riverbank at the bottom of the lane, which handily coincides with the inaugural tasting of last autumn's batch of cider. I tend to cook the saddle of a rabbit differently from its legs, which I will often freeze when making this dish for a slow braise or confit at a later date. The lean saddle loin meat favours a quick flash in the pan then a short roast to keep the rabbit tender and succulent.

Cider-roasted rabbit saddles with ramsons & game chips

Serves 4

For the game chips:

200g floury potatoes, such as Maris Piper

1½ litres vegetable oil

4 rabbit saddles

2tbsp plain flour

200ml cider

200ml game stock

2tsp crab apple jelly (see recipe on page 145, replacing medlars with crab apples)

small handful of ramson leaves and flowers, chopped

1 For the game chips, peel and thinly slice the potato (approximately 2mm thick), then rinse in a couple of changes of cold water. Heat a saucepan of vegetable oil to 150C, dry the potato slices with kitchen paper and fry in small batches until golden and crisp. Transfer to kitchen paper – sprinkle over a good pinch of sea salt when cooled.

2 Preheat the oven to 200C(180C fan), Gas 6. Roll the rabbit saddles in seasoned flour, then fry in a hot, oiled frying pan until golden. Transfer to a metal roasting tray along with the cider and game stock, then roast for 6-8 minutes. The rabbit should be firm and when it's ready a metal skewer inserted into the centre of the meat will be hot to the touch.

3 Remove the rabbit from the pan and cover with kitchen foil. Stir the crab apple jelly into the pan juices and bubble on the hob until reduced and thickened. Spoon the reduction over the meat – serve with game chips and a sprinkle of chopped ramson leaves and flowers.

For me, calves' livers represent a good entry-level foray into offal for the tentative dinner guest or family member. Cooked well they have a subtle flavour, with tender pink meat that seems not entirely dissimilar to steak. The addition of sweet apple, crispy sage and sharpness from a spoonful of balsamic shallots makes for a memorable light lunch or supper.

Pan-fried calves' livers with balsamic shallots, apple & crispy sage

Serves 4

8 shallots

olive oil

2tsp brown sugar

1 bay leaf

a few sprigs of fresh thyme

75ml balsamic vinegar

bunch of fresh sage leaves

500g calves' liver

2 garlic cloves

a splash of calvados

2 Cox's apples

To serve:

4 slices of sourdough bread, toasted

1 Preheat the oven to 200C(180C fan), Gas 6. Peel, trim and halve the shallots, then toss in a little olive oil with the sugar, bay leaf and thyme. Tip into an oven-proof dish and roast for 15 minutes – giving them a stir half-way through the cooking time. Add the balsamic vinegar and return to the oven for a further 10 minutes. Set to one side while you cook the meat; they might need a quick warm when you come to plating up. Now fry the sage leaves in a thin layer of olive oil until crispy, then transfer to kitchen paper to soak off any excess oil.

2 Cut the liver into 4 steak-sized portions; they're more manageable and easier to cook this way. Brush with oil, season and sear in a hot pan with the garlic for 1-2 minutes on each side, until just-pink in the middle. Transfer to a plate, cover with foil and leave to rest for 10 minutes.

3 Peel, core and roughly chop the apples, then de-glaze the pan with a splash of Calvados, and toss them through on a reasonably high heat for a few minutes (they want to be heated through with a hint of colour, but retaining a bit of crunch). Meanwhile, toast the sourdough slices and then serve the liver, apples and shallots on top with a scattering of crispy sage leaves.

This is perfect winter fare – a few smoked mackerel fillets flaked into the bowl wouldn't go amiss if you fancy something a touch more substantial.

Pearled spelt with apple, broccoli & hazelnuts

Serves 4

200g pearled spelt

200g tenderstem broccoli

75g hazelnuts, skin on

handful of baby kale leaves

2 eating apples

50g rye crackers, smashed into small pieces

For the dressing:

juice of ½ an orange

1 tbsp cider vinegar

3 tbsp rapeseed oil

salt and pepper

1 Rinse the spelt well. Transfer to a saucepan, cover with water and bring to the boil. Simmer for 20 minutes, until the spelt is soft but al dente. About mid-way through the cooking time, place a metal sieve or colander over the bubbling pan, tip in the broccoli and cover with the saucepan lid to steam. Lift off the broccoli (careful when removing as the metal is likely to be hot), drain the spelt and set both aside to cool.

2 Toast the hazelnuts in a dry heavy-bottomed pan until taking on a bit of colour and fragrance and then roughly chop them. Core the apple and cut into matchsticks, then toss together with the spelt, broccoli, kale, nuts and rye crackers.

3 Mix the dressing ingredients together and toss through the salad just before serving.

Mignonette is a classic French oyster dressing, given an orchard-twist here with the inclusion of sweet, crunchy apple. Take the upmost care when shucking oysters; if you're worried about tackling them ask your fishmonger to 'pop' the shells for you, which is essentially the first stage of the shucking method below – the hinge twist.

Oysters with apple mignonette

Serves 4

12 fresh oysters

3 shallots, finely chopped

1 small eating apple, finely chopped

80ml red wine vinegar

Kit:

shucking knife

1 To shuck the oysters: place an oyster, rounded-side down on a sturdy work surface. Wrap a thick tea towel around your non-knife-hand, hold the oyster down and carefully insert the tip of the blade of a shucking knife into the hinge. Give it a twist; when the shell gives, push it into the oyster and run the blade along the inside of the top shell to cut through the joining muscles. Remove the lid, then slide the knife underneath the oyster to separate it from the base shell – careful not to spill any of the tasty oyster juices. Repeat with the remaining oysters.

2 Stir the chopped shallots, apple and vinegar together in a small bowl. Spoon over the prepared oysters just before serving, then finish with plenty of freshly cracked black pepper.

Fresh scallops, seared briefly in a scorching hot pan, cool apple, sweet crab apple jelly and earthy truffle – this ticks a multitude of boxes on the flavour front. I often serve the scallops singularly in their shells as a hot canapé, but this recipe also works plated up as a starter with 3-4 scallops per person, with a handful of crunchy watercress leaves on each plate and crusty bread to share.

Pan-fried scallops with apple, crab apple jelly & truffle

Serves 12 as a hot canâpé or 4 as a starter

4tsp crab apple jelly (see recipe on page 145, replacing medlars with crab apples)

1 eating apple

juice of 1 lemon

12 fresh hand-dived scallops, roe on or off (depending on personal preference)

1 summer truffle

If serving as a starter:

watercress

crusty bread

1 To make the crab apple jelly, follow the exact same recipe as Medlar jelly on page 145, simply replacing medlars for crab apples.

2 Core the apple, then use a mandolin to cut into approximately 3mm slices. Use a knife to cut into matchsticks, then transfer to a small bowl. Squeeze over the juice of ½ the lemon and toss lightly. Set to one side.

3 Pat the scallops dry with kitchen paper and season with salt and pepper. Heat a heavy-bottomed frying pan, then add a splash of olive oil. When the oil is hot, add the scallops one-by-one. Think of the pan as a clock face; start at 12 and place clockwise in a circle (if they're spaced evenly, the final scallop should land at around 11). After 2 minutes start flipping the scallops – start at 12 as before. This process helps you keep track of when each went in to ensure an even cooking time; leave them on the heat for 1 further minute. Take off the heat and squeeze over the juice from the other half of lemon. Serve with the apple matchsticks, crab apple jelly and a grating of fresh truffle.

There is an alternative way of making cider vinegar using chopped apples, but in the spirit of thrift I like this way of using leftover scraps. Sadly, it's not recommended to use home made vinegar for pickling; a minimum acetic acid level of 5% is needed to protect against harmful bacteria in the long term – without specialist kit it's not possible to test acidity levels at home (it's likely that your batch will clock in at about the 1-2% mark). Regular use of cider vinegar (1-2 teaspoons, stirred into a glass of water) may help manage blood sugar levels, boost healthy bacteria in the gut and aid digestion. The same process works for both pears and quinces - this vinegar will keep in the fridge for a few months.

Apple cider vinegar

apple peelings and cores
(how much you need depends on
the size of jar that you are using)

½tsp granulated sugar

water

1 Loosely fill a sterilized jar with leftover apple peelings and cores. Try not to pack them in too much; there'll be less room for water, which in turn equates to a smaller batch of vinegar. Sprinkle in the sugar, then fill with water until the peelings are covered. Cover the jar with a piece of muslin and leave in a dark, warm spot for 3-4 weeks.

2 Quite early on in the process a greyish film should start to form on the top of the liquid. Don't worry; this is known as the 'mother' and forms as a by-product of the fermentation process. This can be skimmed off the surface with a spoon and discarded, or used as a starter for further batches of vinegar. Taste the liquid for sharpness from about week three onwards; if it lacks a vinegary bite leave it to ferment for another week or so. Remove the peels and cores, strain the vinegar through a coffee filter to remove any sediment and bottle.

I love making granola. I also love the fact that once the basic elements are in place (oats, nuts, honey and oil), I can pretty much freestyle with the fruit additions. I've stuck to dried apples, raisins and cherries in this instance, but any dried fruit will work.

Orchard granola

200g porridge oats

25g whole almonds

25g whole walnuts

25g whole hazelnuts

25g pumpkin seeds

15g poppy seeds

75ml honey

50ml sunflower oil

50g dried apple slices

50g raisins

50g dried cherries

1 Preheat oven to 180C(160C fan), Gas 4. Mix the oats, nuts, pumpkin seeds and poppy seeds together in large bowl, then stir in the honey and oil. Line a baking tray with parchment paper and then spread the mixture evenly and thinly onto it. Bake for 10-15 minutes until golden.

2 Leave to cool, then break up into small clumps. Toss through the apple slices, raisins and cherries, then serve with cold milk. The granola will keep for a month in a tightly sealed container.

This dessert has real wow-factor; it's easy to make and can be entirely prepped ahead. Simply warm the poached apples before serving and plate up with the candied hazelnuts and toffee sauce.

Cider-poached apples with toffee sauce & candied hazelnuts

Serves 6

For the poached apples:

1 litre cider (roughly equates to 2 average-sized bottles)

150g light brown sugar

1 cinnamon stick

1 star anise

zest of 1 lemon

6 eating apples

For the candied hazelnuts:

50g granulated sugar

100g roughly chopped hazelnuts

25g butter, melted

1 egg white

For the toffee sauce:

300ml pot of double cream

100g light brown sugar

75g butter

a few drops of vanilla essence

1 Heat the cider, sugar, spices and lemon zest in a pan, stirring occasionally until the sugar has dissolved. Peel the apples and spoon carefully into the hot cider. Bring the spiced cider to the boil, then turn the heat down and simmer for further 20 minutes, or until a sharp knife slips easily through the flesh of an apple. Take the pan off the heat and let the apples cool in the liquid.

2 Preheat oven to 190C(170C fan), Gas 5. To make the candied hazelnuts, whisk the egg white for a minute or so until frothy, then gently fold in the granulated sugar, hazelnuts, most of the butter and a pinch of salt. Lightly grease a baking sheet with the leftover butter, then spread over the mixture. Bake for 5-7 minutes until golden; a watchful eye is recommended as it can burn pretty sharpish. Let it cool before breaking it up into little pieces.

3 Gently melt the cream, sugar, butter and vanilla essence together in a pan. Bring to a low bubble and keep stirring until the liquid is a thick, golden toffee colour. Serve warm, plated with a poached apple and a sprinkle of candied nuts. For extra decadence, a spoonful of calvados cream is a worthy addition.

Discovery has to be one of my favourite eating apples. It's an early one; I've picked them in late July after long, hot summers and found them to be perfectly ripe. The flesh has a vibrant magenta blush when cut, while the taste is crisp, sweet and refreshing in the still heat of a sun-baked afternoon in the orchard. Discovery is a natural partner for sticky toffee and works brilliantly in this baked cheesecake recipe – good eaters like Cox or Braeburn are more than worthy alternatives if you're unable to find them.

Baked toffee apple cheesecake

Serves 8-10

200g ginger biscuits

75g butter

6 discovery apples

600g cream cheese

100ml double cream

150g caster sugar

50g plain flour

vanilla essence

For the toffee sauce:

300ml pot of double cream

100g light brown sugar

75g butter

a few drops of vanilla essence

Kit:

A 23cm spring-form cake tin

1 Grease a baking tin with butter and line with parchment, then blitz the biscuits in a food processor until fine and tip into a bowl. Melt the rest of the butter and add. Spread the biscuit mix onto the bottom of the tin; use the back of a spoon to flatten it out into an even layer. Put in the fridge to chill.

2 Preheat oven to 180C(160C fan), Gas 4. Peel, core and finely chop two of the apples. Whisk the cream cheese, double cream, caster sugar, flour and vanilla essence together, then stir in the chopped apple. Pour the mixture over the biscuit base and bake for 30-40 minutes, after which the centre of the cheesecake should have a uniform wobble when gently shaken. Turn the oven off and leave the cheesecake in the oven until it has cooled.

3 To make the toffee, melt the cream, sugar, butter, a pinch of salt and a few drops of vanilla essence together in a pan. Bring to a low bubble and keep stirring until the liquid is a thick, golden toffee-colour. Spoon a thin layer of toffee onto the cheesecake. Core, slice and arrange the remaining 4 apples on top. Use a pastry brush to thinly coat the apple slices with toffee (this will create a seal and stop them going brown). Drizzle over the remaining toffee before serving.

A decent tarte tatin is one of the cornerstones of the orchard repertoire; I've made countless variations over the years, but this has to be my favourite. The rum can be replaced with Calvados and the results are equally enjoyable, although it does compromise the pleasingly alliterative recipe title somewhat...

Russet & rum tarte tatin

Serves 6 conservatively,
4 if you're feeling indulgent

4 Russet apples

60g golden caster sugar

40g light soft brown sugar

50g butter

50ml dark rum

150g puff pastry

1 Preheat the oven to 200C(180C fan), Gas 6. Peel, core and halve the apples. For the caramel, melt the sugar on the hob in a heavy bottomed, 20cm oven-proof pan. Keep a watchful eye on the sugar; when it starts to smoke take the pan off the heat and stir in the butter and rum. Mix through quickly and thoroughly.

2 Turn the heat down, return the pan to the hob and cook the apples in the caramel for 5 minutes or until they start to soften slightly. Arrange the apples curved-side down in the pan and set to one side (off the heat).

3 Roll the puff pastry out thinly and use a 22-23cm plate as a guide to cut out a large pastry circle. Drape the pastry over the apples, tuck the edges in around the fruit and bake for 20-25 minutes, or until the puff pastry is firm and golden. Let the tarte tatin cool for 5 minutes, place a plate on top of the pastry and carefully turn over. Remove the pan and spoon over any leftover caramel. Eat immediately!

I don't think that an orchard cook book would be complete without the inclusion of a decent apple pie. This is my late Nan's recipe, the smell of it alone is enough to take me back to the family Sunday lunches of my childhood. Using self-raising flour means that you can't really prep the pastry too far in advance, but it makes for a wonderfully light, flaky crust.

Classic deep-filled apple & raisin pie

Serves 6

For the filling:

1kg chopped cooking apples

50g raisins

125g golden caster sugar

½tsp ground cinnamon

¼ of a nutmeg, freshly grated

2tbsp plain flour

For the pastry:

250g self-raising flour

125g butter, straight from the fridge and cut into cubes

2tbsp caster sugar

1 egg, beaten

1-2tbsp cold water

To glaze/finish:

1 egg, beaten

2tbsp caster sugar

1 Tip the chopped apples and raisins into a large saucepan, along with the caster sugar, spices, flour and a splash of water to stop the fruit catching on the bottom of the pan. Cook on a medium heat for about 15 minutes until the apple has started to soften. Transfer to a bowl and sit in the fridge to cool completely.

2 For the pastry, blitz the flour and butter in a food processor until well mixed, with a crumb-like texture. Transfer to a large mixing bowl, stir in the sugar, then add the egg. Use your hands to bring the dough together; it'll probably need a tbsp or 2 of cold water to help it bind. Wrap the dough in cling film and pop it in the fridge for 20 minutes before using.

3 Preheat the oven to 190C(170C fan), Gas 5. Cut off roughly two thirds of the pastry, roll it out and line a 25cm pie dish (approximately 3cm deep), allowing for a bit of pastry overhang at the edges. Spoon in the apple filling, then roll out the final third of pastry into a 25cm-round. Brush the pastry rim with a little water, then use a rolling pin to drape the pastry lid over the top of the pie. Trim the edges with a knife, then use a fork to press all the way around the pastry lid.

4 Brush with egg, sieve over 1 tbsp of caster sugar and bake for 40-45 minutes until golden. Leave to cool for 10 minutes, then dust with the remaining sugar.

It's cold, wet and windy outside – the perfect excuse for a bit of baked apple roulette with a clutch of different varieties from the orchard. It's only when you cook these apples together that you realize quite how different they are. This recipe requires you to make the boozy damson gin mincemeat a month ahead, but it is well worth it.

Baked apples with boozy damson gin mincemeat

Serves 6

Boozy damson gin mincemeat (prepare a month ahead):

200g unsalted butter

200g light muscovado sugar

½ tsp ground cinnamon

good grating of fresh nutmeg

600g mixed dried fruit (I used roughly equal parts raisins, currants and sultanas)

1 large Bramley apple peeled, cored and grated

zest and juice of 1 large orange

150ml damson gin

6 eating apples, mixed or single variety

4tbsp damson gin mincemeat (see recipe above)

25g unsalted butter

3tsp demerara sugar

1 cinnamon stick

100ml damson gin or port

Kit:

glass jars

1 To sterilize the jars, heat the oven to 140C(120C fan), Gas 1. Wash the jars in hot soapy water, then rinse off under the tap. Remove the rubber seals and put the jars onto a baking tray and then leave until dry in the oven. (Use boiling water to sterilize any rubber seals, as they will dry out and crack if put in the oven.)

2 To make the boozy damson gin mincemeat, slowly melt the butter in a large pan; take off the heat and stir in the sugar, cinnamon and nutmeg. Mix the dried fruit, grated apple, orange zest, orange juice and damson gin together in a separate bowl (it's good to do this the night before if you get a chance). Stir the butter into the fruit, mix together well and spoon into the sterilized jars. Leave the mincemeat to mature for at least a month before using.

3 Heat the oven to 180C(160C fan), Gas 4. Core the apples, score around the circumference of each with a small, sharp knife and arrange in an oven-proof dish. Divide the mincemeat between the apples, using a fingertip to push the mixture into each piece of fruit. Top with a small knob of butter and ½ tsp of sugar, then pour the damson gin into the bottom of the dish. Nestle in the cinnamon stick, then bake for 20 minutes, or until the apples are soft (this really depends of the type of dessert apple that you're using). Serve each apple with a spoonful of cooking liquor.

There's a gentle pace about making and baking sourdough. In terms of hands-on time it doesn't feel particularly labour intensive, it's more the slower proving time that requires a bit of patience and time management. We eat this bread warm from the oven with plenty of mature cheddar – the cider really comes through and gives the bread a lovely chewy texture.

Cider sourdough

Serves 8

For the levain:

2tbsp sourdough starter

50g white bread flour

50g warm water

For the loaf:

500g white bread flour

300g warm cider

10g fine salt

1tbsp olive oil

rice flour for dusting

1 Mix together the levain ingredients, cover with a tea towel and leave in a warm place until bubbly, elastic in texture and yeasty/tangy to smell – I usually start mine just before going to bed and leave it overnight.

2 The next morning add the remaining flour, cider, salt and oil. Bring together into a ball of dough and knead on a floured surface for 10 minutes.

3 Give a large bowl a brush with olive oil and sit dough inside. Cover loosely with clingfilm and leave in a warm spot for 3-4 hours.

4 Knock the risen dough back by punching it a few of times. Turn it out onto a floured surface and gather it up into a neat round. Dust a proving basket with rice flour, nestle the dough inside (smooth side facing down), then cover with a tea towel and leave until doubled in size.

5 Preheat the oven to its hottest setting (about 240C, Gas 9 is preferable). Transfer the dough to an oven-warmed 20cm cast-iron casserole dish. Slash the top a few times with a razor blade, pop the lid on and bake for 35 minutes. Resist the temptation to have a look at it for this initial period – the intense, enclosed environment is an integral part of a good rise.

6 Remove the lid, lower the oven to 220C(200C fan), Gas 7 and bake for a further 10-15 minutes. Remove from the oven and transfer to a cooling rack; once it has cooled slightly give the underside a tap – if it sounds hollow the bread is baked properly. Leave to cool for 20 minutes before slicing.

Pears

Pears

I often remind myself of an old English proverb when I'm in the orchard – 'You plant pears for your heirs'. There's no denying that a pear tree can take time to produce a crop; planting a fruit tree is by no means a purely altruistic endeavour, but one can't escape the sense that these trees will be enjoyed by others in years to come.

Pears, in addition to apples, cherries, plums, quinces and medlars, are members of Rosaceae, a family of flowering plants that also includes roses, blackberries, meadowsweet and hawthorn. The first mention of the pear is to be found in Homer's *Odyssey*, where they are outlined as one of the gifts of the gods, alongside apples and figs. Pears have retained a continued association with opulence throughout history, with early references ranging from Tang Dynasty China (618-907AD) where they were treated as a delicacy, through to seventeenth-century France, where they were considered to be the fruit of royalty. Louis XIV's gardeners grew around fifty varieties of pear in the *Potager du Roi* (King's Kitchen Garden) near the Palace of Versailles; it's thought that one of the trees in that garden is the ancestor of today's Comice pear.

It's all about timing with pears. They won't ripen on the tree, but need to be picked at just the right moment. Hold a pear by the base, then gently tilt it upwards so that it hangs horizontally. If the stalk breaks away from the tree without a tug, it's ready. It's important to chill pears in the fridge for a week or so before transferring to a fruit bowl; this period in cold storage really makes for a better flavour when ripe. A gentle squeeze at the point where the stalk joins the fruit is a good check for ripeness; if the pear flesh yields without having to apply too much pressure, you've caught it at its best.

Pears often play second-fiddle to apples. The fact that you can't just pluck a pear off a tree and eat one, plus the brief window of optimum ripeness are likely to be contributing factors. I can't get enough of them; if anything their slight awkwardness makes it all the more rewarding when you get it just right.

I use slightly under-ripe pears in this recipe; they need the briefest of simmers in the curry towards the end – retaining a bit of crunch is key. This is fresh, vibrant and lifts the spirits on a cold winter's day when the fruit trees are bare and spring seems a lifetime away.

Chicken & pear Thai curry

Serves 4

150g green beans, trimmed

400g chicken (breast or thigh)

coconut oil

2 garlic cloves, chopped

1 lemongrass stalk, tough outer layer removed and thinly sliced

2 Kaffir lime leaves

thumb-sized piece of galangal, peeled and sliced

1 bird's eye chilli, kept whole but scored lengthways with a sharp knife

2tbsp green curry paste

400ml coconut milk

100ml chicken stock

150g Thai pea aubergines

a stalk of young green peppercorns

2tsp fish sauce

3 pears

juice of 1 lime

To serve:

Thai basil leaves

Thai sticky rice

1 Bring a pan of water to the boil and cook the green beans for 3 minutes. Drain and set to one side.

2 Chop the chicken into similar-sized chunks. Heat a splash of coconut oil in a wok or large frying pan, then fry the meat on high until nicely browned all over. Turn the heat down to medium and stir in the garlic, lemongrass, lime leaves, galangal and chilli; give them a minute to soften then add the curry paste, coconut milk, stock, pea aubergines, peppercorns and fish sauce. Bring to a bubble.

3 Let the curry simmer for 5 minutes. Meanwhile core and slice the pears and add along with the green beans, season and cook for a further 3 minutes. Stir in the lime juice just before plating up and serve with extra lime wedges, a scattering of Thai basil leaves and some sticky rice.

Sweetcorn and pear make for an unusual but favourable acquaintance. This feels like a late summer dish – the chicken thighs could be cooked on the barbecue if the weather's fine.

Jerk-spiced chicken thighs with pear & sweetcorn salsa

Serves 4

For the chicken:

2tsp allspice berries

1tsp ground cinnamon

1tsp chilli flakes

¼ nutmeg, freshly grated

2tsp dried thyme

1tsp dried parsley

1 garlic clove, roughly chopped

1tsp sea salt

2tsp black peppercorns

1tsp muscovado sugar

1tbsp rapeseed oil

8 plump chicken thighs, skin scored

For the salsa:

1 ripe pear, peeled, cored and chopped

2 shallots, finely chopped

1 red chilli, de-seeded and finely chopped

1 sweetcorn cob, charred on a barbecue or griddle pan

juice of 2 limes

small bunch of mint leaves, chopped

1 Blitz the spices, herbs, garlic, salt, pepper, sugar and oil in a food processor until smooth. Rub the chicken thighs with the mixture – use your hands to work it in so that the meat is completely covered. Sit the meat in an oven-proof tray covered with cling film and leave in the fridge for a minimum of 2-3 hours to marinade.

2 Heat oven to 220C(200C fan), Gas 7. Bake the chicken for 35-40 minutes until crisp and cooked through – drain off any fatty pan juices intermittently.

3 Stir the pear, shallots, chilli, sweetcorn, lime juice and mint together in a small bowl, then spoon over the chicken thighs just before serving.

A rare, indulgent treat, worth getting spot-on. I find leaving the rind to air-dry in the fridge after a brush with vinegar gives a better crunch; moisture is the nemesis of the pork scratching.

Pork scratchings with fennel seeds & pear sauce

Serves 8

For the pork scratchings:

500g good quality pork rind

1 tbsp cider vinegar

2 tsp sea salt

1 tsp fennel seeds, roughly pounded in a pestle and mortar

For the pear sauce:

2 ripe pears

1 tbsp granulated sugar

small knob of butter

1 Brush the pork rind lightly with cider vinegar, then leave to air-dry in the fridge – ideally overnight if possible.

2 Preheat the oven to 240C (220C fan), Gas 9. Cut the rind into 5cm x 2cm strips, then toss in a bowl with the salt. Arrange on a shallow baking tray and roast for 20-25 minutes, turning halfway through and carefully removing any scratchings that look ready while the others finish off. Let the scratchings cool and then sprinkle with the fennel seeds.

3 Peel, core and roughly chop the pears. Tip into a small pan with the sugar and butter and cook on a medium heat for 15 minutes until the fruit has softened. Take off the heat and roughly mash with a fork; I like to retain a bit of texture and the occasional rogue chunk of pear so try not to make it too smooth.

It's not just the name that makes this feel right for a bonfire or firework party. The mix of sticky, sweet, savoury and a pop of heat from the mustard is exactly the kind of thing you want to be eating on a cold November night; fire blazing, scarves done up tightly and sparklers at the ready.

Sticky honey & mustard Catherine wheel sausage with pears, cobnuts & celeriac mash

Serves 4

For the celeriac mash:

750g celeriac, peeled and roughly chopped

100ml hot milk

50g butter

6 spring onions, chopped

For the sausage and pears:

a string of 12 good quality pork chipolatas (make sure that they're joined together)

3 ripe pears

knob of butter

small wine glass of dry perry or cider

1 tbsp wholegrain mustard

2 tbsp honey

To serve:

100g fresh cobnuts, chopped

Kit:

2 wooden skewers, soaked in water

1 Tip the celeriac into a large saucepan and cover with water. Add a pinch of salt and bring to the boil – simmer for 20 minutes until tender, then drain. Return the cooked celeriac to the pan and mash roughly. Stir in the hot milk, butter, spring onions and some seasoning then mix well. Pop the lid on the saucepan and keep warm until the sausages are ready.

2 Untwist the links between the chipolatas and push the sausage meat up towards one end to make one long sausage. Roll the sausage into a spiral and push a couple of wooden skewers through at right angles to secure.

3 Halve the pears and take out the cores with a melon baller. Fry the sausage in a large frying pan on a medium heat for 10 minutes on each side until browned all over. Drop a good knob of butter into the pan, then add the pears. After 5 minutes, stir in the perry/cider, mustard and honey – season, then pop a lid on the pan and simmer on low for 15 minutes, turning the pears and sausage intermittently. Serve with a scattering of chopped cobnuts and the celeriac mash on the side.

Pear juice adds a nice fruity pop to this sweet and sour brine. Make sure that your fish is fresher than fresh when sousing; the initial heat will seal the outside of the mackerel fillets in the short term, but it's the day spent slowly curing in the sousing liquid that gives the mackerel it's texture and flavour.

Soused mackerel with pear juice, rhubarb & ginger

Serves 4 as a starter

decent chunk of root ginger

2 shallots

200ml pear juice

150ml cider vinegar

1 star anise

1 tbsp caster sugar

1 tsp salt

75g rhubarb

4 fresh mackerel fillets, bones removed

To serve:

4 slices of dark rye bread, toasted

1 Peel and thinly slice the ginger and shallots, then add to a large hob-proof roasting dish with the pear juice, vinegar, star anise, sugar and salt. Bring to the boil; roughly chop the rhubarb, add to the pan and continue to simmer for another couple of minutes.

2 Use a fish slice to carefully lay the mackerel fillets flesh-side down in the hot pickling liquid (check them over beforehand for any rogue bones with a pair of tweezers), then keep on a medium heat for a final 3 minutes. Remove the dish from the heat, let it cool to room temperature, cover with cling film and leave in the fridge for 24 hours.

3 Drain the fillets from the liquid and serve with slices of toasted rye bread.

Pickled pears are one of my winter storecupboard must-haves; ideally made a few days in advance, they'll brighten up even the simplest of cheeseboards and are a great way of preserving a glut of fruit.

Chicory, stilton & pickled pear salad

Serves 4 as a starter

For the pickled pears:

500ml cider vinegar

300g sugar

zest of 1 lemon

1tsp black peppercorns

pinch of saffron strands

1kg pears - Maltese variety Bambinella taste great as well as looking pretty on the plate, but if you can't find these just use any ripe pear, peeled, cored and quartered.

For the salad:

4 chicory heads

4 wedges of blue cheese, crumbled

50g hazelnuts, skin on

2tsp linseeds

50g dried cherries

For the dressing:

3tsp olive oil

2tsp of the pickling liquor

juice of ½ a lemon

Salt and pepper

Kit:

sterilized jars

1 For the pickled pears, heat the vinegar, sugar, lemon zest, peppercorns and saffron in a pan. When the sugar has dissolved tip in the pears and simmer for 10-15 minutes until tender. Leave to cool in the pickling liquor, then decant the pears into sterilized jars, along with their pickling liquid.

2 For the salad, cut the base off the chicory heads and remove the leaves. Arrange on plates with a couple of pickled pears, then crumble over the blue cheese.

3 Roughly chop the hazelnuts then toast with the linseeds in a heavy-bottomed pan for a few minutes until golden and fragrant. Scatter over the plates, along with the dried cherries.

4 Mix together all the dressing ingredients – spoon over just before serving and savour with biscuits or crackers.

Lockets restaurant was a regular haunt for politicians during the 1970s, situated within shuffling distance of Westminster on Marsham Street. This simple, eponymous menu favourite is essentially posh cheese on toast, but merits a mention as the combination of peppery watercress, sweet pear and tangy Stilton is such a winner.

Lockets savoury

Serves 4

4 slices of crusty white or brown bread (I use a nice rye sourdough)

handful of watercress leaves

2 pears

200g Stilton

I Toast the bread, then arrange a small bunch of watercress leaves on each slice (snip off and discard any thick stems). Half and core the pears, then cut into approximately ½cm slices. Arrange the pear slices on top of the watercress, then cover with a few slices of Stilton. Pop under the grill for a minute or two, then serve hot with a pinch of salt and a good grind of black pepper.

Half of my family hail from Germany and I've eaten plenty of great German cakes over the years – a good Nusskuchen is hard to beat. Each autumn, I contemplate the naïve romantic notion of gathering my own hazelnuts from the hedge of coppiced hazel that leads into the orchard; I've yet to get there before the squirrels.

Pear Nusskuchen

Serves 8-10

100g hazelnuts, plus a few whole ones to decorate

200g unsalted butter

200g caster sugar

4 eggs, plus two egg whites

200g plain flour

4 tbsp milk

1 tsp baking powder

4 tbsp strong coffee

7 pears

2 tbsp caster sugar

1 star anise

300ml double cream

icing sugar, to decorate

1 Preheat oven to 180C(160C fan), Gas 4. Grease and line two 20cm cake tins. Blitz the nuts in a food processor until fine. Cream the butter and sugar together with an electric whisk until pale and fluffy, then whisk in the 4 eggs one at a time. With a spoon, mix in the nuts, flour, baking powder and coffee.

2 Whisk the 2 egg whites in a separate bowl until they form stiff peaks, then carefully fold into the cake mixture with a metal spoon.

3 Divide the mixture equally between the lined cake tins, then bake for 25-30 minutes until golden and a skewer comes out cleanly from the centre of the cakes. Leave to cool for 10 minutes, then transfer to a wire rack.

4 Turn the oven down to 140C(120C fan), Gas1. To make some dried pear slices for the decoration, firstly cover a baking sheet with parchment, then thinly slice 3 of the pears and spread them on the sheet. Bake for one hour, flipping the slices halfway through. Set aside to cool.

5 Peel, core and chop the remaining 4 pears, then add to a pan with 2 tablespoons of caster sugar, a splash of water and the star anise. Simmer on low for 20 minutes or so (depending on how ripe your pears are) until the pear has softened but not dissolved to a purée. Cool before using.

6 To assemble, whisk the double cream until thick, then spoon over the base cake layer. Spoon a layer of the cooked pears on top of the cream, then top with the second cake layer. Arrange the dried pear slices on top of the cake with a few whole hazelnuts, then dust with icing sugar.

The arrival of autumn always catches me unaware. All too often it's as if summer has hit its stride, when suddenly it starts to drain from the tips of leaves with quickening haste. The branches of the Black Worcester (or Warden) pear are particularly colourful, a riot of red, purple and orange. Hot saffron and red wine-baked pears would have been commonplace on city streets during Shakespeare's time; the Worcester pear is even referenced in A Winter's Tale: *'I must have Saffron to colour the Warden Pies'. Warming, delicately spiced and comforting.*

Warden pears baked with red wine, saffron & spices

Serves 4

500ml red wine

100g golden caster sugar

1 cinnamon stick

pinch of saffron

¼tsp ground ginger

4 Black Worcester pears (any just-ripe pear will work excellently)

crème fraîche, to serve

1 Pour the wine into a small saucepan and bring to a simmer along with the sugar and spices. Take off the heat once the sugar has dissolved.

2 Preheat the oven to 200C(180C fan), Gas 6. Peel the pears; nestle on their sides in an ovenproof dish and pour over the spiced wine. Bake for 20-30 minutes, or until a sharp knife slips easily through a pear – make sure to turn them every now and again so that they are evenly coated. Serve in bowls with a drizzle of the cooking liquor and plenty of crème fraîche.

This is the perfect pud; warm, rich, fruity and a just little boozy.
It's pretty easy to make, using mostly storecupboard ingredients
– a good one to have on standby when you need to turn a dessert
around quickly.

Pear & date pudding

Serves 4

150g Medjool dates

wine glass-full of brandy

50g raisins

zest and juice of ½ an orange

85g butter, softened

85g light brown sugar

2 eggs

1 tsp vanilla essence

140g self-raising flour

1 tsp bicarbonate of soda

1 tbsp caster sugar

1 large pear

1 Roughly chop the dates, then tip into a food processor with the brandy and orange juice. Pulse briefly a few times – you're after a roughly textured consistency, but nothing too smooth. Peel the pear, then cut a cheek off one of the sides. Set the cheek to one side, core and chop the remaining pear and stir into the blitzed dates, along with the raisins and orange zest. Leave for a couple of hours to soak.

2 Heat oven to 180C(160C fan), Gas 4. In a bowl whisk the butter, sugar, eggs and vanilla essence together until pale and fluffy, then beat in the flour and bicarbonate of soda. Fold in the date mixture.

3 Butter a pudding bowl, then spoon in 1 tbsp of caster sugar. Angle the bowl and tap, rotating as you do so that the sugar sticks to the butter. Discard any excess sugar. Slice the pear cheek about ten times, taking care not to cut all the way through to the stalk end. Fan out the slices and place flat-side down at the bottom of the bowl. Spoon over the pudding mixture, then bake for about 40-50 minutes, or until a skewer comes out clean from the centre of the pudding. Serve with hot custard.

It's impossible to forget a Stargazey pie if you've ever seen one. Cornish in origin, it's a traditional savoury dish of baked sardines, eggs and potatoes, complete with fish heads poking through the pastry to (supposedly) look up wistfully at the stars. Oddly enough, it's the inspiration for this dessert, but without the sardines of course. In my sweetened version, pears have the astronomical inclination – I love the way that the rhubarb dyes the plump base of each pear with a blush of pink.

Peargazey patchwork pie

Serves 6

6 pears

200g caster sugar

1 vanilla pod, cut in half lengthways

400g rhubarb, cut into 4cm chunks

2tbsp golden caster sugar

150g shortcrust pastry

1 egg, beaten

2 tbsp demerara sugar

Kit:

pizza wheel

1 Nestle the pears in a saucepan and cover with water. Stir in the caster sugar and vanilla then bring to a simmer. Let the pears bubble away for about 10 minutes or until a knife just about slips through the flesh. Remove the pears from the liquor (keep this for the time being) and set aside to cool.

2 Once cooled, cut the bottom off each pear flat so that they stand upright. Arrange in the bottom of a deep 23cm-round pie dish, as equally spaced apart as possible. Toss the rhubarb in the golden caster sugar and spoon around the pears. Drizzle a tablespoon of the pear poaching liquor over the rhubarb.

3 Heat the oven to 190C(170C fan), Gas 5. Roll the pastry out onto a flour-dusted surface and use a pizza wheel to cut irregular-shaped-but-similar-sized-patches. Cover the rhubarb with the pastry shapes, arranging between the upright pears and overlapping to seal the crust and create a patchwork effect. (See the photograph on page 2.)

4 Brush the pastry with beaten egg and sprinkle over the demerara sugar. Bake for 30-35 minutes until the pastry is golden – cover the pears with kitchen foil if you're worried that they might catch.

Choose the ripest pears that you can find for this Chelsea bun filling, the balance of sweet and sticky is spot-on.

Pear & raisin Chelsea buns

Makes 7 buns

For the filling:

2 pears, peeled cored and chopped

100g raisins

75ml Calvados or pear brandy

35g butter, softened

50g soft brown sugar

For the dough:

220ml full-fat milk

45g butter

400g white bread flour

7g fast-action dried yeast

45g golden caster sugar

10g fine salt

1 egg, beaten

To bake/glaze:

1 egg, beaten

3tbsp sieved apricot jam

3tsp demerara sugar

1 To make the filling: tip the pears, raisins and Calvados into a small bowl and set aside to soak.

2 To prepare the dough gently warm the milk in a pan, then stir in 50g of butter; once it has melted remove from the heat. Mix the flour, yeast, caster sugar and salt together in a large mixing bowl, then stir in the warm milk and beaten egg. Tip the dough onto a floured surface and knead for between 5-10 minutes until smooth and elastic. Brush a clean bowl with oil, sit the dough inside and cover with a tea towel. Leave in a warm place to rise until roughly doubled in size.

3 Knock the dough back on a flour-dusted surface, then roll out to a 20x30cm sized rectangle – about the size of an A4 sheet of paper. For the filling use the back of a spoon to spread the softened butter out evenly onto the dough, then scatter over the fruit and brown sugar. Roll the dough into a Swiss roll shape from one of the long sides, then cut into 7 pinwheels. Line a large tray with baking parchment and arrange with a 1cm gap between each bun. Cover with a tea towel and leave for a second prove – until roughly doubled in size again.

4 Heat the oven to 200C(180C fan), Gas 6. Brush the buns with a little beaten egg and bake in the middle shelf of the oven for 20-25 minutes until golden. While the buns are cooling, heat the apricot jam in a small pan until runny, then brush over the Chelsea buns. Sprinkle over the Demerara sugar and leave for 15 minutes before serving. The buns will keep for a few days in an airtight container, but as with all breads you can't beat them just-baked and eaten warm.

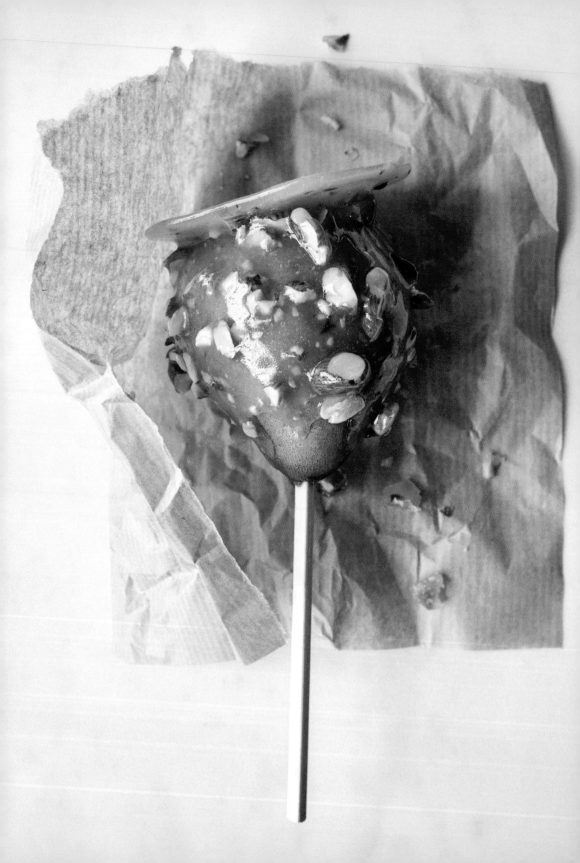

An updated version of a childhood favourite, but one that I'm sure everyone will love. Miso gives the toffee a slightly salty, umami hit; If any of your guests have an aversion or intolerence to the nuts leave them out and sprinkle with mini marshmallows before the toffee sets.

Miso toffee-nut pears

Makes 6

6 ripe pears, preferably a variety with russeted skin such as Taylor's gold

110ml water

220g granulated sugar

25g butter

½tsp cider vinegar

1tsp white miso paste

50g hazelnuts, chopped

Kit:

wooden sticks

sugar thermometer

1 Remove any stalks in the pears, then poke a stick into the top of each and push down to about half-way through.

2 To make the toffee warm the water in a pan, then add the sugar to dissolve. Stir in the butter and vinegar then bring to the boil. You need to heat the toffee to hard-crack stage (150C if you have a sugar thermometer); this takes about 10 minutes, after which a small drop of toffee spooned into cold water will go rock hard and sink to the bottom.

3 Take the toffee off the heat. Stir in miso and nuts. Next line a baking tray with parchment, then hold each pear by the stick and carefully coat in nutty toffee. Stand on the tray and leave to cool.

I love an autumn barbecue, and baking pears in the remnants of a fire is a great way of cooking them. Make sure that the embers aren't too hot, although if the pears catch ever so slightly on the outside it shouldn't really matter – it's the soft baked flesh inside that you're after.

Brown butter doughnuts with ember & bay-baked pears & chocolate sauce

Serves 10

*For the doughnuts
(makes 20 small ones):*

75ml buttermilk

75ml whole milk

7g fast-action dried yeast

60g unsalted butter

250g strong white bread flour

40g caster sugar, plus extra
to coat the doughnuts

1 egg, beaten

1½ litres vegetable oil for deep
frying

For the chocolate sauce:

200g dark chocolate

125ml double cream

75ml whole milk

2tbsp golden syrup

For the pears:

10 ripe pears

6-8 Branches of bay leaves,
approximately 25cm in length,
soaked overnight in water

4tbsp Eau de Vie Poire William

1 Warm the buttermilk and milk in a pan; remove from the heat and stir in the yeast. Set aside for 15-20 minutes. In a separate pan, heat the butter on a medium temperature until it starts to colour; it'll be frothy on top but little brown specks will start to appear on the bottom. Watch it closely – the butter should smell nutty. Take off the heat, transfer to a bowl and leave to cool for about 10 minutes.

2 Sift the flour into a large mixing bowl then add the yeasty milk, butter, caster sugar, egg and a good pinch of salt. Bring together into a dough and knead on a floured surface for 10 minutes. Lightly brush a bowl with vegetable oil, pop the dough in and cover. Leave in a warm place until doubled in size. Knock the dough back, chop into 20 pieces then roll into small balls. Transfer to oiled baking sheets and cover loosely with oiled sheets of cling film. Leave to prove for 30 minutes. Heat the oil to 180C, then fry the doughnuts in batches for 2½ minutes on each side until golden. Transfer to kitchen paper, then toss in caster sugar while they are warm.

3 Melt the sauce ingredients together in a small pan, stirring regularly until you have a shiny, smooth sauce. Wait until the the embers of your fire are glowing; remove the bay branches from the water and pat dry with kitchen paper. Lay a sheet of kitchen foil on a work surface, then arrange 3 or 4 branches in the centre. Sit half of the pears on top, gather the foil up and scrunch together to create a parcel – spoon in 2 tbsp of the Poire William just before sealing. Repeat with the second parcel, nestle into the embers and bake for 30-40 minutes, or until the pears are soft to the touch.

Plums & Cherries

Plums and cherries

Plums and cherries are similar in so many ways; relatives with a shared heritage but born of different personalities. The cherry tree rocks up like a gregarious younger sibling; quick off the mark with a rush of blossom and bearer of the year's first crop – cheerful red fruit that bursts with vibrant sweetness and colour. Plums are altogether more quiet and reserved; ripening later, sometimes sharp and astringent to the taste – purples and blues masked by a soft cloudy bloom. Both are without exception two of my favourite stone fruits.

Cherries and plum are part of the Prunus genus of trees and shrubs, a family that includes peaches, apricots and nectarines. It's no chance affair that almonds work so well with plums and cherries in the kitchen, as they too are part of the Prunus genus. Plum and cherry trees produce drupes, a fabulous word (though not quite as good as drupaceous, I might add). It defines a fruit with a fleshy outer part surrounding a pit or stone, inside of which a seed (or kernel) lies. Plums are thought to be one of the first domesticated fruits, with stones being found in Neolithic sites, while cherries became popular in Europe in the late Middles Ages. They were introduced to England by Henry VIII, then taken to North America by colonists in the late seventeenth century.

The trees (cherry in particular) are the perfect exemplars of the bud-to-branch ethos. One can literally use everything; blossom, leaves, fruit, stones and branches. Fruiting season depends on location; in the northern hemisphere they are a summer crop, whereas in the southern hemisphere the season peaks towards the end of the year. In certain parts of Australia cherries tend to have a greater association with Christmas – perhaps bolstered by their inadvertent adherence to the festive colour palette. Wherever one's growing them the season for both is brief; neither keep particularly well, so the race is on to make the most of them before their time is up.

Serves 4

For the confit duck tacos:

1 tsp cumin seeds

1 tsp coriander seeds

1 tsp ancho chilli flakes

1 tbsp sea salt

1 tsp black peppercorns

4 garlic cloves

1 cinnamon stick, broken into bits

zest and juice of 1 lime

4 duck legs

500ml duck fat

1 red onion, thinly sliced

juice of 2 limes

For the mole sauce:

1 tsp cumin seeds

1 tsp coriander seeds

½ onion, finely chopped

1 garlic clove, grated

½ red chilli, de-seeded and finely chopped

1 tsp ancho chilli flakes

200g tinned chopped tomatoes

100ml chicken stock

40g dried cherries

20g dark chocolate

juice of ½ lime

pinch of cayenne pepper

To serve:

8 taco shells

175g fresh cherries, destoned and quartered

1 avocado, diced

1 small red chilli, de-seeded and thinly sliced

small bunch of coriander

lime wedges

I often confit my duck legs way ahead of eating; submerged in their cooking fat, sealed and kept in the fridge they'll keep for weeks. Either way, they will need to be prepared a minimum of 24 hours in advance.

Confit duck & cherry tacos with quick mole sauce

1 To prepare the confit duck, toast the cumin and coriander seeds in a dry pan until fragrant, then transfer to a pestle and mortar along with the chilli, salt, pepper, garlic, cinnamon and lime. Pound to a paste and rub all over the duck legs. Sit the meat in an oven-proof dish, cover with foil and leave in the fridge for 12-24 hours, turning the legs every now and again.

2 Heat oven to 150C(130C fan), Gas 2. Drain off any juices that the meat may have released; brush off the marinade but leave it in the dish as you pour the duck fat over the legs. Make sure that the duck is completely submerged in fat, then cook in the oven for 2½ hours, after which the meat should feel like it's coming away from the bone easily. Carefully remove the meat from the dish and drain on kitchen paper. Meanwhile, thinly slice the onion, transfer to a small bowl and squeeze over the lime juice – plus a good pinch of sea salt. Stir together and leave to macerate for at least an hour before serving.

3 For the mole, toast the cumin and coriander seeds in a pan as before, crush in a pestle and mortar and set to one side. Soften the onion, garlic, chilli and chilli flakes in a splash of olive oil, then stir in the spices, tomatoes, stock and dried cherries. Simmer on low for 10 minutes. Blitz everything in a food processor until smooth, return to the pan and stir the chocolate through until melted. Kill the heat, stir in the lime juice and cayenne pepper then season to taste. Serve at room temperature.

4 Heat oven to 200C(180C fan), Gas 6. Roast the duck legs for approximately 20-30 minutes, until the skin is crispy. Shred the meat and serve in taco shells with the onions, cherries, avocado, chilli, coriander leaves and mole sauce. Serve with lime wedges.

*These cherries will keep unopened for up to a year; I jar them up in
the summer at the height of the cherry season and see if my willpower
is strong enough to hold off eating until Christmas – they're great with
cheese, charcuterie and game such as venison, pheasant and pigeon.*

Pickled cherries with pink peppercorns & coriander seeds

500g cherries

200ml red wine vinegar

200ml water

125g caster sugar

2tsp pink peppercorns

2tsp coriander seeds

1 bay leaf

1 Cut a cross into each cherry then drop into sterilized jars; I use an assortment of smaller different-sized jars but one single 1-litre jar should do the job.

2 Put the vinegar, sugar and water into a pan, stir in the pink peppercorns, coriander seeds and bay leaf and bring to the boil. Set to one side to cool for 5-10 minutes.

3 Pour the hot vinegar over the cherries, and leave for at least a week before using.

Steak and chips, with a twist. Tkemali is used in Georgian cuisine in a similar way to ketchup. I gather wild cherry plums in late summer and bottle enough to (hopefully) last me through the year. If the cherry plums are a bit thin on the ground, the squint-inducingly tart flesh of a damson is the perfect replacement.

Bavette steak with tkemali & fries

Serves 4

For the tkemali:

1kg wild cherry plums or damsons

2tbsp brown sugar

½tsp dried coriander

4 garlic cloves, chopped

1 red chilli, de-seeded and chopped

handful of fresh coriander

handful of fresh dill

small handful of fresh mint

1tsp salt

For the steak, lettuce and fries:

8 baby gem lettuces, frilly outer leaves removed and cut in half

2tbsp olive oil

juice of ½ a lemon

4 large Maris Piper potatoes

1½ litres vegetable oil, for deep frying

1kg bavette steak

Kit:

sterilized bottles

1 For the tkemali, blanche the cherry plums in a pan of boiling water for a few minutes. Strain, remove the skins and stones then return to the pan. Bring the fruit pulp back to a low simmer, then stir in the sugar, dried coriander, garlic and chilli. Keep on the heat for a further 5 minutes – if it's a bit watery keep it bubbling away for a little while longer until it reduces to the consistency of ketchup. Take the sauce off the heat and let it cool for 10 minutes. Stir in the fresh herbs and salt then blitz in a food processor. Cool the sauce, then bottle.

2 Toss the gem lettuces in a little olive oil, season and place cut-side down on a hot griddle pan or barbecue for a few minutes – keep an eye on them, as they can go too far and burn if left for too long. Leave to cool, then dress with the olive oil and lemon juice.

3 There's no need to peel the potatoes. Use a mandolin slicer to cut into 3cm slices, then chop into matchsticks and spread out onto kitchen paper to absorb any excess water. Heat the oil until hot and starting to smoke; if a test fry dropped into the oil bubbles frantically and cooks to a golden colour in about a minute you're ready to go. Cook in batches, removing from the oil with a slotted spoon and transferring to a tray lined with kitchen paper. Season with sea salt.

4 Make sure that the steak's at room temperature, brush with a little olive oil and season all over with salt and pepper. Fry for 2 minutes on each side, then remove from the heat, cover with kitchen foil and leave to rest for 4 minutes. Slice the steak, then serve with the fries, lettuce and a good blob of tkemali.

Mahleb is an unusual spice made from the ground kernels of the St Lucie cherry. I've a small tree of my own; it is yet to yield fruit (and more importantly, stones), but I hope to be able to produce my own mahleb in the not-too-distant future. In the meantime, the spice is readily available online – this is my version of ka'ak, a popular bagel-like bread ring commonly sold on the streets of Beirut. The taste of mahleb is not dissimilar to almond, with a touch of cherry and a hint of bitterness. These rolls are delicious with falafel and some crunchy pink-pickled turnips.

Lebanese ka'ak rolls with mahleb

Makes 8 rolls

For the bread dough:

500g strong white bread flour

150ml warm water

7g fast-action yeast

1tsp fennel seeds

1tsp green aniseeds

1tsp sesame seeds

10g sea salt

2tsp mahleb powder

150g warm whole milk

1tbsp olive oil

To glaze/finish:

1 egg, beaten

1tsp sesame seeds

1 Mix 50g of the flour, 50ml warm water and the yeast together in a small bowl. Cover with a tea towel and leave in a warm spot until bubbling and yeasty for 30-60 minutes.

2 Toast the fennel, aniseed and sesame seeds in a heavy bottomed pan until fragrant, then transfer to a pestle and mortar, along with the sea salt and mahleb. Grind until fine, then tip into a large mixing bowl with the remaining 450g flour, 100ml water, milk and olive oil. Stir in the bubbling starter and bring the dough together with your hands.

3 Tip the dough out onto a floured surface and knead for 5-10 minutes. Brush a clean mixing bowl with olive oil and rest the dough inside – cover with a tea towel and leave to prove in a warm place until doubled in size.

4 Line 2 trays with baking parchment, then knock the dough back and cut into 8 pieces. Shape into rings – I do this by rolling a piece of dough into a ball, poking a finger through the middle and spinning it around on my finger to enlarge the hole. Sit the rings on the trays – make sure that there's a bit of space between each. Cover again with tea towels and leave to prove again until roughly doubled in size.

5 Heat the oven to 220C(200C fan), Gas 7. Brush the risen rolls with egg and sprinkle with sesame seeds. Bake for 20-25 minutes, or until golden on top, underneath and hollow-sounding when tapped.

I'm a big fan of umeboshi (Japanese salt plums); it feels only natural to have a go at making my own. Make sure you use really sweet plums for salting; the process is essentially a similar idea to that of curing – water is drawn out of the plums over time, leaving dried fruit with a texture like fudge and a sweet/salt plum taste. I slice them thinly and use almost like a seasoning. You'll need 4 salted plums for this recipe but I tend to do a larger batch at the time and use them for other things...

Pan-fried venison with red cabbage, salted plum, caraway & parsnip crisps

Serves 4

(Prepare 4-6 weeks ahead)

For the salted plums:
12 plums, really sweet
sea salt

For the salad and parsnip crisps:
half a red cabbage
4 salted plums (see recipe above)
1 tbsp olive oil
2 tsp red wine vinegar
juice of ½ a lemon
1 tsp caraway seeds
4 large parsnips
olive oil

For the venison:
4 venison steaks
a good knob of butter

1 For the salted plums: sprinkle 2cm layer of sea salt across the bottom of a medium-sized, food container. Nestle the plums on top with a 1cm space between each and cover with more sea salt. Leave for 4-6 weeks until firm.

2 For the salad: thinly slice the red cabbage, de-stone and slice the plums. Toss together with the olive oil, vinegar, lemon juice, caraway seeds and some salt and pepper.

3 For the parsnip crisps, preheat the oven to 180C(160C fan), Gas 4. Top, tail and thinly slice the parsnips, then toss in a bowl with olive oil. Arrange on a baking tray and cook for 20-25 minutes, flipping halfway through the cooking time and whipping out any smaller crisps that look ready ahead of the others.

4 Season the venison steaks, brush a hot pan with olive oil and fry on one side for 2 minutes. Turn the steaks over and fry for a further 2 minutes, adding the knob of butter a minute in and basting the steaks for the final 60 seconds. Leave to rest for 3-4 minutes before serving.

*A pan of comfort, spice and warmth to sit in the centre of the table
– dive in and serve with plenty of sticky rice.*

Ginger & soy pork with plums

Serves 4

2 tbsp seasoned flour

splash sesame oil

1kg pork shoulder, cut into 4cm pieces

250ml ginger beer

thumb-sized piece of root ginger, finely chopped

3 garlic cloves, finely chopped

1 red chilli, de-seeded and thinly sliced

500ml chicken stock

5tbsp soy sauce

1 cinnamon stick

1 star anise

6 plums, halved and de-stoned

2tsp sesame seeds

To serve:
sticky rice

1 Preheat oven to 160C(140C fan), Gas 3. Toss the pork in seasoned flour, then heat a splash of sesame oil in a non-stick ovenproof pan until hot and fry the meat until nicely browned. You may need to do this in batches, and add a little more oil.

2 De-glaze the pan with a splash of ginger beer, then stir in the ginger, garlic and chilli. Soften for a few minutes, then stir in the meat (plus any juices left on the plate), stock, soy sauce, cinnamon stick, star anise and remaining ginger beer. Cover the pan with either a lid or kitchen foil and cook for 2 hours, stirring every now and again for the first hour and a half. Add the plums for the final 30 minutes, but try not to stir from now on (spoon juices over instead); it's easy to accidentally mash up the softening plums if you mess with it too much.

3 Toast the sesame seeds in a heavy bottomed pan until golden, then sprinkle over the pork and plums. Serve with sticky rice.

The orchard is contemplating the onset of winter as I gather damsons this afternoon. The somewhat regally titled 'king of the damsons' (also known as Bradley's King) is a late cropper; fortuitously for me the stones of this variety fall away from the flesh easily – unlike most damsons that I've encountered in the past. Damsons are naturally sharp; sugar and spice balances acidity. This sauce teams up perfectly with rich, gamey duck and cool ribbons of cucumber.

Five spice duck with damson relish

Serves 4

small piece of fresh root ginger, grated

½ red onion, thinly sliced

zest and juice of 1 orange

200g damsons

4tbsp caster sugar

1 star anise

splash of cider vinegar

3tbsp Chinese five spice powder

4 duck breasts, skin on

To serve:

small cucumber, thinly sliced lengthways

4 spring onions, cut into strips

1 Gently soften the ginger, onion and orange zest in a small pan while you de-stone the damsons. Stir in the fruit, sugar, star anise, orange juice and vinegar, then cook for a further 10 minutes (if your damsons are a bit on the sharp-side you may have to add a little extra sugar along the way). Leave to cool.

2 Spoon the five spice powder onto a large plate, then add a good pinch of salt and pepper. Score the skin on each duck breast with a sharp knife, then roll in the spice mix.

3 Fry the duck breasts in a little groundnut oil skin-side down for 7-10 minutes until the skin is crispy. Turn and cook for a further 5-7 minutes. Rest for 10 minutes, then serve with the thinly sliced cucumber, spring onions and a good dollop of the damson relish.

I love mochi. This traditional confectionary is known as wagashi in Japan, eaten mostly in late March when the sakura, or flowering cherry tree, comes into bloom and is celebrated during the viewing festival of hanami. The distinct fragrance of the leaves is enough to transport me to Tokyo in spring.

Sakura mochi

Makes 12 mochi

For the pickled cherry leaves:

2tbsp fne salt

4tbsp boiling water

12 young cherry leaves (allow 2 days for soaking)

bowl of iced water

For the azuki bean paste:

125g dried azuki beans soaked overnight

125g caster sugar

For the rice:

200g glutinous rice soaked overnight

400ml water

drop of pink food colouring

50g caster sugar

1 Fot the pickled cherry leaves, stir the salt and boiling water together and leave to cool. Blanche the leaves in a pan of boiling water for 10-15 seconds, then transfer to a bowl of iced water. Sit the leaves in a small dish, pour over the brine and refrigerate for 2 days. Drain, pat dry with kitchen paper and store in an airtight sandwich bag. Soak the leaves in cold water before using.

2 Rinse the rice and azuki beans separately in a few changes of cold water, then leave to soak overnight. Drain the rice, then add to a microwaveable bowl with the water and the food colouring. Cover tightly with cling film, microwave for 3 minutes, stir, re-cover and cook for a further 3 minutes. Discard the film, cover with a cloth and leave to cool for 5 minutes. Stir in the sugar and use a pestle to pound until semi broken-down and sticky.

3 For the paste, drain the beans, cover with water in a small saucepan and bring to a simmer. Cook for 45 minutes, topping up the water as-and-when. When the beans have softened enough to crush easily, strain and blitz in a food processor. Return the pulp to the pan, stir in the sugar, a pinch of salt, a splash of water and simmer on low (stirring regularly) for 20 minutes until the mixture is thick. Leave to cool, then divide the bean paste into 12 portions (about 25g each). Dip your hands in cold water and roll each into a small ball.

5 Roll out a sheet of cling film and spritz with a little water. Take a twelfth of the rice (about 55g) and flatten into a circular pancake on the film – sit a bean paste ball in the centre. Scoop up the cling film and gather the pancake around the ball; twist the ends of the film, tighten and roll on a work surface so that the bean paste ball is completely sealed inside the rice. Remove the film, flatten slightly with the palm of a water-dipped hand and wrap in a cherry leaf. Repeat for remaining mochi.

*Frozen morello cherries work best for the cherry mousse as they
retain their vibrant colour when cooked – also this is a cake for
spring, when delicate cherry blossom gathers on the tips of sakura
branches and the thought of a fresh cherry is a distant one.*

Cherry, matcha & sakura mousse cake

Serves 8

For the cake:

100g butter

100g caster sugar

2 eggs

85g plain flour

15g matcha green tea powder

1 tsp baking powder

For the cherry mousse:

3 leaves of sheet gelatine

600g de-stoned frozen morello
cherries

3 egg whites

150g caster sugar

300ml double cream

To decorate:

icing sugar

cherry blossom (optional)

1 Heat the oven to 180C(160C fan), Gas 4. Whisk the butter
and sugar together until fluffy, then beat in the eggs. Sieve in
the flour, matcha powder and baking powder, then beat again
until you have a thick batter. Line a 20cm loose-based cake tin,
pour in the mixture and bake for 25 minutes, or until a skewer
comes out clean when poked into the top of the cake. Transfer
to a wire cooling rack with the bottom of the cake facing upwards.

2 Fot the mousse: soften the gelatine sheets in a bowl of cold
water for 5 minutes. Tip the frozen cherries into a pan and
bring to a gentle simmer. Blitz to a purée, pass through a sieve
and then add the gelatine. Stir until it has dissolved, then set
aside to cool to room temperature (but don't refrigerate).

3 Wash and re-line the cake tin with cling film, allowing for a
generous overhang all the way round. Sit the cake on a work
surface, this time the right way up. The cake should have a
domed top; two level tiers of sponge are needed here though
so use a bread knife to trim off the curved top and make the
cake level. Cut the levelled cake into two equal-sized discs,
then put the top half into the lined tin.

4 Whisk the egg whites until light and fluffy, then whisk in the
sugar bit-by-bit until thick, glossy and forming stiff peaks. Whip
the cream in a separate bowl until it starts to thicken, then
fold into the meringue with the cooled cherry mixture. Pour
the pink mousse over the sponge base, level with the back of
a spoon and then top with the other half of sponge (with the
bottom of the original cake facing upwards). Gather the cling
film up over the cake and refrigerate for a minimum of
3 hours before serving – overnight if possible. To serve, dust
with icing sugar and decorate with cherry blossom.

My Eton mess is less of a mess in the traditional sense. The core elements are all here though. In this instance I like to pipe the meringue into little droplets rather than smash up a larger meringue. Add rosewater conservatively: start with half a teaspoon at a time, as strengths vary between brands and you don't want to overdo it.

Cherry & rose Eton mess

Serves 4

2 large egg whites

150g caster sugar

400g cherries, de-stoned

300g double cream

1 tsp icing sugar

1 to 2 tsp rosewater

To serve:

fresh rose petals

Kit:

piping bag

1 Heat the oven to 120C(100C fan), Gas 1. Whisk the egg whites in a large mixing bowl until they reach stiff peaks, then gradually whisk in 125g of the caster sugar, until you have glossy stiff peaks. Use a teaspoon to press a small blob of meringue into the four corners of a large baking tray, then cover with baking parchment (the meringue will stick the paper down and stop it rolling up). Fill a piping bag with the meringue and pipe small blobs onto the parchment, pulling the bag up quickly after squeezing each to give the tops a little peak. Bake for 10-15 until the meringues are crisp on the outside, then turn off the heat and let the meringues sit in the cooling oven for 30 minutes before removing.

2 Stir roughly a third of the cherries and the remaining 25g of sugar together in a small saucepan with a splash of water. Heat to a low bubble – keep on the heat until the cherries have softened. Leave to cool for 10 minutes, then pass through a sieve into a small bowl. Set to one side to cool completely.

3 Whisk the double cream with icing sugar until it starts to thicken – careful not to over-whisk. Then mix in the rosewater. To serve, lightly fold the cherry syrup into the cream to streak with pink. Stir in three-quarters of the meringues and fresh fruit and spoon the mix into bowls. Finish with a scattering of the remaining cherries, meringues and rose petals.

I wouldn't advise making these on the night – i.e. grappling with a spaetzle maker in the kitchen while your dinner guests polish off the last of the damson gin in your absence. Spaetzle are great fun to make, but can be a touch on the fiddly-side. There's absolutely no reason why you can't make the little dumplings in advance, leave them on a tray in the fridge (covered with a sheet of cling film) and sauté in the clarified butter just before serving.

Kirschspaetzle

Serves 4

250g plain flour

1tsp ground cinnamon

good grating of fresh nutmeg

4 eggs

50ml milk

2tbsp clarified butter

splash of kirsch

200g fresh cherries

1tbsp caster sugar

To serve:

crème fraîche

ground cinnamon

1 Mix the flour, cinnamon, nutmeg and a pinch of salt together in a large bowl. Whisk the eggs separately and beat into the dry ingredients. Gradually stir in the milk, loosening the flour-egg mix to a thick batter. Set aside for 10 minutes.

2 Bring a pan of water to a gentle simmer. Push the dough through a spaetzle maker or large-holed colander into the water. Cook for 5-7 minutes until they start to float; you'll need to cook the spaetzle in batches so remove each batch with a slotted spoon, drain and spread out on a large plate or tray (don't pile them up or they might stick together).

3 Melt the butter and kirsch in a frying pan and stir in the spaetzle. Fry on a medium heat for 10 minutes, or until the spaetzle have taken on a bit of colour. Soften the cherries in a separate pan with the caster sugar; stir into the buttery spaetzle and serve hot with crème fraiche and a dusting of cinnamon.

For me this is the taste of late summer holidays in France; sweet wine perfumed with lavender and honey, thickened to a syrup to coat a bagful of cheerful yellow plums from the market. There's a Mirabelle tree in the orchard, but I actually find them quite a bit when I'm out and about on my foraging travels.

Mirabelle plums simmered in rosé wine with lavender & honey

Serves 4

300ml sweet rosé wine

4tbsp honey

500g Mirabelles or similar cherry tomato-sized plums

a few sprigs of fresh lavender

To serve:

double cream

chopped cobnuts (optional)

1 Bring the wine and honey to a gentle simmer, then stir in the plums and lavender. Leave to bubble for 5 minutes until softened (the Mirabelle skins may split but this isn't the end of the world); remove the fruit from the liquid with a slotted spoon and set aside.

2 Taste the syrup for a quick lavender check; if the flavour is a bit feint leave it in for a short while longer but be careful not to overdo it. Remove the lavender and reduce the liquid by two-thirds until thickened and darker in colour.

3 Warm the plums through in the syrup for a few minutes before serving. Serve with a good dollop of double cream, a drizzle of syrup from the pan and finely chopped cobnuts.

*These sugar plums are so simple to make and require only five ingredients,
but honestly – the flavour is astounding. I came across the seeds of the
rather wonderfully named Pimpinella anisum by chance, but they have
become a firm favourite in the kitchen. Plum and aniseed is such a good
pairing – serve on toasted brioche with scoops of vanilla ice cream.*

Sugar plums with green aniseed

Serves 6

½tsp green aniseed

150g granulated sugar

1 egg white

12 ripe plums

butter, for greasing

To serve:

slices of brioche, toasted

vanilla ice cream

1 Use a pestle and mortar to grind the aniseeds until fine,
then pass through a small sieve into a bowl (this avoids any
husks making their way into the flavoured sugar). Stir in the
sugar and set to one side.

2 Heat the oven to 200C(180C fan), Gas 6. In a large mixing
bowl whisk the egg white until frothy but still translucent. If
you've got stiff peaks in the bowl you've gone way too far. One
by one, dip the plums into the egg white – hold above the bowl
for a few seconds to drain off any excess white, then roll in
the sugar (a pinch sprinkled on top is handy for filling any gaps).

3 Grease a large baking dish with butter, then arrange the plums
inside with a bit of space between each. Bake for 15 minutes.
Serve with slices of toasted brioche and vanilla ice cream.

It's a brief season for greengages, so it pays to make the most of them while they're at their best. A bowl of emerald green Reine Claude greengages sitting on the kitchen table brightens up the greyest of days. They lose their colour a touch when cooked, but are rightly considered to be one of the finest plums.

Greengage & pistachio cobbler

Serves 6

750g greengages, de-stoned and halved

good squeeze of honey

zest of ½ an orange

½tsp ground cinnamon

150g caster sugar

60g pistachios (shelled)

200g self-raising flour

75g unsalted butter, grated

125ml whole milk

1 Preheat the oven to 190C(170C fan), Gas 5. Tip the greengages into an ovenproof dish, then cover with with the honey, zest, cinnamon and 50g of the sugar. Give it all a gentle shake, then pop in the oven to warm while you make the topping.

2 Using a food processor, blitz 50g of the pistachios to a fine consistency. In a large bowl, mix together the flour, ground nuts and remaining 100g of sugar. Add the grated butter, then use your fingertips to gently rub everything together into a fine, breadcrumb-like mix. Stir in the milk to form a thick, doughy batter.

3 Roughly chop the remaining nuts then take the fruit out of the oven. Spoon large blobs of the cobbler mix on top, scatter with the pistachios and bake for 30-40 minutes (or until nicely browned and a skewer comes out of the topping clean).

Quinces & Medlars

Quinces and medlars

The beauty of the blossom alone is enough to tempt you into planting a quince or medlar. There are two quince trees in the orchard (pear-shaped and Vranja); their late-season flowers often remind me of magnolia, a delicate sweep of white, flushed with soft pink at the edges. The two medlars (Royal and Nottingham) are equally striking, with star-like blossom and long oval leaves that take on every red and gold hue imaginable in the late autumn sun. Both are related to apples and pears, but are rather less than forthcoming when offering up their culinary secrets. One mustn't be put off; all they want from us is a little bit of time and patience to bring out their potential – who doesn't – the rewards to the perseverant cook are many.

Quinces are rock-hard when picked; they also taste quite bitter and shouldn't be eaten raw. The fragrance of an uncooked quince is a different affair; a bowlful sitting on a kitchen table will fill the room with a gorgeous floral, almost honey-like scent. The best way to cook a quince is to peel it, half it and slip it into a just-bubbling pan of sugar syrup for an hour or so – the fruit slowly softens and starts to turn a deep, ruby pink. Once cooked, they'll sit submerged in the syrup in the fridge for at least a week. Quince-infused syrup is almost as useful an ingredient in the kitchen at the fruit itself, so make sure that you keep hold of it.

Medlars, on the other hand, are an altogether stranger fruit. They taste a bit like a cross between dates and apple sauce; there are hints of custard in there – maybe even a touch of cinnamon. They are also hard and practically inedible when picked off the tree – they need to be bletted before they can be used in the kitchen. Placed apart on a well-ventilated work surface for a couple of weeks, the fruit starts to break down internally. When they are soft to squeeze, they are ready to use.

In terms of the trees themselves, quince and medlars require a little less TLC than apples and pears pruning-wise once they're established, but there can be issues. Quince are prone to blight, which can affect cropping and often comes about during wet summers. This isn't an issue with medlars, but it's worth keeping an eye out for moth caterpillars in spring, who have something of a penchant for the young leaves. Both fruits are much-loved and versatile additions to my kitchen; I use them regularly in savoury and sweet dishes. Quinces keep well too; I once found a couple in storage that I'd overlooked in the spring (it was summer by this point) they were still rock-solid and hadn't spoiled a bit.

Membrillo has been around in varying forms across the world since as early as fifth century Rome, although in recent times it's most commonly associated with Spain. The basic principle is roughly the same wherever it's made; quince purée and sugar are cooked until thick, then cooled to a firm paste. I use membrillo all the time in the kitchen – it's great to add a subtle sweet note to gravys, softened with honey to glaze a Christmas ham or served simply on a cheeseboard with chunks of Manchego cheese.

Membrillo

1kg quinces

granulated sugar (equal to the weight of your pulp)

Kit:
ramekins or moulds

1 Roughly chop the quinces; there's no need to peel or core them. Add to a large pan, then fill with water until the fruit is just about covered. Bring to the boil then turn down to a low bubble; stir regularly until the quince pieces are soft enough to squash when pressed against the side of the pan with a spoon. Remove from the heat and leave to cool for an hour or so.

2 Pass the mixture through a sieve; the slender offerings of pulp coming through might seem alarming at first, but it doesn't take long to fill a small bowl. Weigh the pulp and return to the pan with an equal amount of sugar.

3 Let the pulp and sugar bubble away on a medium heat; stir regularly so that it doesn't catch on the bottom of the pan. It will start to thicken gradually; you'll know it's ready when a wooden spoon can be swiped across the bottom of the pan and it takes a couple of seconds for the mixture to run back into the furrow. Pour into jars or moulds (a ramekin works well in the absence of a mould) and leave to cool.

It sounds rather strange to pair sweet quince with garlic, but I assure you this works – it was something of a revelation when I first tried it. Quince aoli is often served with tapas in Spain; I find that it's the perfect accompaniment to crispy squid, served hot from the pan with a pinch of paprika and a few peppery rocket leaves.

Crispy squid with quince aoli

Serves 4

For the aoli:

3tbsp good quality mayonnaise (if homemade, even better)

50g quince poached in sugar syrup, plus 1tbsp of syrup (see page 131)

1 garlic clove, chopped

For the crispy squid:

3 medium squid, cleaned and cut into 1cm rings. Keep the tentacles too.

50g plain flour

50g cornflour

1tsp paprika

½tsp cayenne pepper

vegetable oil, for frying

To serve:

paprika

fresh rocket leaves

lemon wedges

1 To make the aoli, blitz the mayonnaise, quince, syrup, garlic and a pinch of salt in a food processor until smooth, then transfer to a serving bowl.

2 For the crispy squid, mix the flour, cornflour, paprika, cayenne and some seasoning together in a bowl, add the squid and toss lightly with your hands to coat the squid all over.

3 Heat the oil to roughly 180C; a test with a cube of bread should brown in half a minute when dropped in. You need to cook the squid in batches; fry for a minute or so until crisp and golden then drain on kitchen paper. Serve with a sprinkle of salt, paprika, rocket leaves and lemon wedges.

These sausage rolls are great for a picnic, or a somewhat snazzy lunchbox. Lamb and quince are natural partners, while a cool minty dip is a lovely contrast to the warmth and spicing of the sausage rolls.

Moroccan lamb & quince sausage rolls with mint & yoghurt dip

Makes 8 sausage rolls

For the sausage rolls:

2 white onions

1 red chilli, de-seeded and chopped

2tsp dark brown sugar

175g cooked quince, diced (see page 131)

1tsp fennel seeds

1tsp cumin seeds

½tsp coriander seeds

½tsp smoked paprika

1tsp sumac

1tsp ras-el-hanout

2tsp harissa paste

1tsp salt

1tsp black pepper

600g lamb mince (20% fat)

320g puff pastry

1 egg, beaten

For the yoghurt dip:

150g natural yoghurt

small handful of fresh mint leaves

1 garlic clove

juice of ½ a lemon

splash of olive oil

1 Grate the onions and squeeze between your hands to get rid of any excess water. Heat a splash of olive oil in a frying pan, then sweat the onions, chilli and sugar on a low heat for 20 minutes. Set aside to cool.

2 Warm the fennel, cumin and coriander seeds in a heavy-bottomed pan for a few minutes, then crush to a rough paste in a pestle and mortar along with the paprika, sumac, ras-el-hanout, harissa paste, salt and pepper. Mix the spice paste, onions, lamb and quince together in a large mixing bowl, using your hands to make sure that all of the elements are well combined.

3 For the dip: blitz the yoghurt, mint, garlic, lemon juice and oil in a food processor. Season to taste.

4 Roll the puff pastry out to roughly a 25cm x 20cm rectangle, then arrange the lamb mix in a sausage shape across the longest side, about 2-3cm from the bottom edge of the pastry. Brush the 2-3cm gap with some of the beaten egg, then lift the other side of the pastry over the sausage meat. Press the pastry edges together to seal, then cut the strip into 8 sausage rolls. Chill in the fridge before baking.

5 Preheat the oven to 200C(180C fan), Gas 6. Brush the sausage rolls with the remaining egg and bake for 25-30 minutes. Serve warm with a final sprinkle of ras-el-hanout.

One of those dishes that pretty much cooks itself after a bit of initial prep; browning the meat gives depth of flavour, while the slices of quince soften gently in the pan juices for the latter part of the cooking time.

Slow–cooked lamb with quince

Serves 6

750g lamb neck fillet, cut into 4-5cm pieces

2tbsp plain flour

splash of damson gin
(see page 173)

2 medium red onions, cut into wedges

2 cloves of garlic, chopped

1 bay leaf

1tsp ground cumin

1tsp ground coriander

good grind of fresh nutmeg

5 cardamon pods

1 cinnamon stick

pinch of saffron

zest of 1 lemon

600ml lamb stock

3 quinces, peeled, cored and cut into eighths

To serve:

pomegranate seeds

couscous

1 Heat the oven to 160C(140C fan), Gas 3. Toss the lamb lightly in the flour, then heat a splash of oil in a pan until hot and cook the meat in batches until nicely browned. Transfer to a large oven-proof dish.

2 De-glaze the frying pan with the damson gin, then add to the lamb dish along with the onion, garlic, bay leaf, spices, lemon zest and stock. Pop a lid on the dish and cook in the oven for 3 hours or until tender, stirring the quince slices in 45 minutes from the end of cooking time. Serve with a sprinkle of pomegranate seeds and couscous.

This is pretty much cheese-lovers' nirvana; cutting open a baked Camembert is one of those moments that compels a collective gasp around the table, before a quick clamour to find a suitable means of damming the tide of melted cheese. Roasted garlic cloves can be squeezed and spread onto toast before diving in.

Puff pastry baked–Camembert with quince & roasted garlic

Serves 4

375g pack puff pastry

1 quince poached in sugar syrup (see page 131)

1 egg, beaten

poppy seeds

To serve:

1 garlic bulb, roasted

4 slices toasted sourdough

1 Heat the oven to 200C(180C fan), Gas 6. Lightly flour your work surface and roll the pastry out to a 5mm thickness. Cut out two circles; the base should be about the size of a saucer (the cheese needs to have about a 2-3cm gap all the way round), while the top should be the size of a dinner plate.

2 Lay your hand flat on top of the Camembert and use a serrated knife to carefully cut the cheese in half horizontally (a bit like how you'd cut a cake in half). Slice the quince and arrange evenly on top of the bottom half of the cheese. Put the top lid of the cheese back on. At this point it's a good idea to use a sharp knife to trim the sharp-edged top of the rind off, so that the cheese has a nice dome shape when covered.

3 Cover an oven-proof tray with a sheet of baking parchment. Put the smaller pastry circle in the middle, then carefully place the filled-cheese on top. Brush the exposed pastry at the base with egg, then lift the pastry lid on. Shape the pastry around the cheese with your hands, then use a fork to pinch the pastry seam together and create a seal. Brush with egg, scatter some poppy seeds over the top and bake for 25 minutes until golden. Serve with roasted garlic cloves and toasted sourdough.

Arrope can trace its origins back to a time when the Moors occupied the Iberian Peninsula – the name is derived from the Arabic Arrúbb (meaning dense, thick stew). Fresh grape juice is reduced to a concentrated syrup, after which it's traditionally used to preserve fruit such as quince, pumpkin, figs and plums. It's good to keep the leftover quince and sugar syrup from this recipe in the fridge, or make extra batches, as there are plenty of other uses for it in this chapter.

Sticky pumpkin & arrope puddings with quince

Serves 6

For the quince poached in sugar syrup:

2 large quinces, peeled, cored and halved lengthways

750ml water

100g sugar

3tbsp honey

juice of ½ lemon

For the arrope:

2 litres pressed red grape juice (not from concentrate)

For the puddings:

75g soft brown sugar

50g butter, at room temperature plus extra for greasing

1 egg, beaten

100g arrope, plus extra for drizzling

125g cooked pumpkin, mashed

125g self-raising flour

½ tsp mixed spice

¼ tsp bicarbonate of soda

50ml milk

3 large figs, halved

300g red grapes, on their stalks

1 quince poached in sugar syrup (see above)

Kit:
6 small dariole moulds

1 For the poached quince (illustrated on the back cover), tip the fruit into a medium-sized pan and cover with the water. Stir in the sugar, honey and lemon juice, then bring to a simmer. Keep on the heat for 60-90 minutes, or until the quinces and syrup have turned pink – cooking time will vary depending on the quinces. Leave to cool and transfer with the syrup, into a large sterilized jar.

2 For the arrope, bring the grape juice to the boil, then reduce by approximately 80%, leaving about 250ml of thick, sticky syrup. Be careful that the liquid temperature doesn't rise above 110C when nearing the end of the process; it quickly becomes toffee if it gets too hot. Set aside to cool.

3 Preheat oven to 180C(160C fan), Gas 4 and butter 6 small dariole moulds. Whisk the sugar and butter together until slightly creamy, then add the egg – continue whisking until pale and fluffy, then beat in the arrope and pumpkin. Mix the flour, mixed spice, a pinch of salt and bicarbonate of soda together in a separate bowl, then fold this gradually into the wet mix along with the milk – be careful though not to overbeat the batter.

4 Spoon the mixture into the moulds, leaving a 1cm gap between batter level and rim. Sit spaced apart on a baking tray, then arrange the figs and grapes around the moulds. Bake for 20-25 minutes until the puddings are risen and firm and the fruit is bubbling. Leave to cool for a few minutes. Use a melon baller to scoop out balls of quince, then plate up with the warm puddings, roasted fruit and a drizzle of arrope.

There's something luxurious about the combination of quince, saffron, pistachio and rose; rich colours and flavours inspired by the riads of Morocco. This ice cream incorporates the poached quince on page 131. It is smooth, creamy, fruity and the perfect way to end an evening meal.

Quince & saffron ice cream with pistachio & dried rose petals

Serves 8

For the ice cream:

300ml double cream

300ml full-fat milk

pinch of saffron strands

100g golden caster sugar

4 egg yolks

2 large quince poached in sugar syrup (see page 131)

To serve:

50mml of the quince poaching syrup

50g pistachios, finely chopped

2tsp dried rose petals

Kit:

bowl of ice

ice cream maker

1 Heat the cream, milk and saffron in a heavy-bottomed pan until it starts to boil; remove from the heat and leave to sit for 15 minutes. Sieve into a bowl and discard the saffron.

2 Whisk the egg yolks and sugar in a large bowl until pale and fluffy. Pour in the warm cream mixture, a little at a time while whisking continuously. Return to the pan and stir the custard on a low heat for about 10-15 minutes until thickened – make sure that it never erupts into a boil. When the custard is thick enough to coat the back of a wooden spoon, remove from the heat and leave to cool for a few minutes.

3 Blitz one of the quinces in a food processor before passing the purée through a sieve. Stir the purée into the custard, ensuring that it's mixed in well. Chop the second quince into small chunks and stir that in too.

4 Fill a large mixing bowl with ice, then snuggle a smaller bowl in among the cubes (make sure that it's big enough to contain your ice cream). Pour in the custard and leave in the fridge to cool. Use an ice cream maker to churn the cold custard until it's thick and scoopable, then transfer into a tub or container. Cover with a lid or cling-film, then freeze – the ice cream will keep for up to three months in the freezer.

5 Reduce the quince poaching syrup in a small pan on the hob by roughly a half, then set aside to cool. Serve scoops of the ice cream with a drizzle of syrup, finely chopped pistachios and a pinch of dried rose petals.

Quinces are full of anthocyanins, natural colour pigments that are bound up in tannins. In their uncooked state, tannins contribute to a fruit's astringency, making them bitter and unpalatable – the introduction of heat and acid (in this instance orange juice) breaks the cells down. It never ceases to amaze me when a quince slowly transforms from a nondescript, pale yellow to a vibrant peachy-pink when cooked; a similar chemical process turns the leaves of trees red in late autumn, which is just about the right time to be making this delicious dessert.

Quinces roasted in Pineau des Charentes with Chantilly cream

Serves 4

For the roasted quince:

200g granulated sugar

4 quinces, peeled and halved

zest and juice of 1 orange

2 wine glasses of Pineau des Charentes (use port or a sweet sherry if you can't get hold of this)

4tbsp honey

1 cinnamon stick

For the Chantilly cream:

150ml double cream

1tbsp icing sugar

seeds from ½ a vanilla pod

1 In a pan, dissolve the sugar in 1½ litres of water. Add the quinces and orange juice, cover and simmer for 25 minutes.

2 Preheat the oven to 200C(180C fan), Gas 6. Arrange the quinces in a large baking dish, then add the wine, orange zest, honey and cinnamon. Cook in the oven for about an hour, turning the quinces regularly and spooning the juice over the softening fruit so that it doesn't dry out.

3 For the Chantilly, whisk the cream, icing sugar and vanilla seeds together until thickened and forming soft peaks. Serve with the roasted quince and a drizzle of the cooking liquor.

I could probably write you a dozen recipes that involve quince and honey, such is the divine bond between the two. This would still be up at the top of the pile; it's best served warm with crème fraîche.

Quince, orange & honey cake

Serves 6

For the cake:

1 quince, poached in sugar syrup (see page 131)

175g caster sugar

175g butter, at room temperature

3 eggs

125g self raising flour

1 Tsp baking powder

50g ground almonds

zest of 1 orange

For the syrup:

100ml quince syrup (leftover from poaching)

1 tbsp honey

juice of ½ an orange

1 Prepare the poached quince by following step one in the recipe on page 131.

2 Cream the butter and sugar together until pale and fluffy, then whisk in the eggs. Fold in the flour, baking powder, almonds and orange zest.

3 Preheat oven to 180C(160C fan), Gas 4. Grease a deep, 20cm spring-form baking tin with butter then line with a disc of baking parchment. Cut the quince lengthways into 8 slices, arrange on top of the parchment, then spoon over the cake mixture. Bake for 30-40 minutes, or until a skewer comes out clean from the cake.

4 Let the cake cool for 10 minutes, then carefully turn out onto a plate. Reduce the quince syrup in a small saucepan by about a half, then stir in the honey and orange juice. Spoon over the cake while the it's still warm (let it cool too much and the syrup won't soak in as well).

These marshmallows take on a gentle pink hue from the quince poaching liquor, while roughly chopped fruit stirred into the un-set meringue brings little pops of intense flavour. There's something Turkish delight-like about the sweet, floral notes of quince; I never tire of making these confections.

Quince marshmallows

Makes 25 marshmallows

200g quince poached in sugar syrup, finely chopped (see page 131)

100g icing sugar

100g cornflour

10 sheets of leaf gelatine

200ml of the quince poaching syrup

200ml water

350g granulated cane sugar

4 large egg whites, at room temperature

Kit:

sugar thermometer

deep 22cm-square tin

1 Prepare the poached quince, following step one in the recipe on page 131. Then finely chop the fruit and set to one side. Mix the icing sugar and cornflour together in a small bowl. Brush the tin with vegetable oil, then line with parchment. Brush lightly with a little more oil, then sieve over the icing sugar and cornflour mix – make sure that the sides of the tin are covered as well as the base.

2 Put the gelatine leaves in a large bowl of cold water to soften while you make the marshmallow. Pour the quince syrup, water and sugar into a saucepan. Stir on a medium heat until the sugar has dissolved, then turn the heat up. The syrup needs to reach firm ball stage (about 125C), so test with a sugar thermometer regularly as the temperature rises. Be patient as this takes a little while.

3 Whisk the egg whites to stiff peaks in a large mixing bowl as the syrup nears temperature. Whisk the syrup into the egg whites, pouring in a steady stream but not too slowly, as the syrup will start to set in the pan when taken off the heat. Whisk for a few minutes until thick and glossy.

4 Remove the gelatine from the bowl and squeeze out any excess water. Whisk the sheets into the mixture one by one; after about 10 minutes the un-set meringue should be really thick but still pourable.

5 Move quickly with the next step – the marshmallow begins to set with a startling degree of haste. Fold the chopped quince into the marshmallow, making sure that it's mixed through evenly. Pour the marshmallow into the tin, level with a spatula and leave to set for 2-3 hours. Cut into 25 cubes and toss in the remaining icing sugar and cornflour.

There are some great things to be foraged among the trees, hedges and wild areas that surround the orchard. Marjoram appears in the same spot near the Black Worcester pear every year; I've had parasol mushrooms by the crab apple, sorrel tucked in behind the two quinces and little clumps of violets that pop up around the base of the wild cherry plum each spring. The flavour of violet is unique; quince is a natural partner with its floral notes, while a slightly bitter chocolate biscuit keeps the sweetness in check.

Chocolate biscuits with quince curd & crystallized violet flowers

Makes 16 biscuits

For the quince curd:

2 large quinces

150g caster sugar

juice of 1 lemon and a couple of strips of zest

75g unsalted butter

3 eggs and 1 egg yolk

For the biscuits:

125g butter

125g caster sugar

2tbsp golden syrup

a few drops of violet essence

50g cocoa

1tsp bicarbonate of soda

250g plain flour

splash of milk

For the crystallized violets:

small bowl of violet flowers

1 egg white

1tbsp caster sugar

Kit:

sterilized jars

1 Preheat the oven to 160C(140C fan), Gas 3. To make the quince curd line a tray with tin foil and bake the quinces for 1½ – 2 hours until soft. Leave to cool, then remove the skin and cores. Blitz the pulp in a food processor, then pass through a sieve.

2 Put the pulp and caster sugar into a heavy-bottomed saucepan and bring to a semi-fast bubble, stirring regularly until the mixture has thickened so that when you drag a wooden spoon through the purée the furrow will close up after a second or two. Squeeze in the lemon juice.

3 Turn the heat down to low, then whisk in the butter. At this point I let the mixture cool a little and pass it through a sieve again, to minimize the chance of a grainy curd. Beat the eggs and yolks together in a bowl, then slowly whisk into the quince pan. Keep on low for 5-10 minutes until thickened, making sure that it never erupts into a boil. Set aside to cool for about 10 minutes, then spoon into sterilized jars.

4 For the biscuits, melt the butter in a saucepan before transferring to a mixing bowl. Leave to cool for a few minutes, then beat in the sugar, golden syrup, violet essence, cocoa and bicarbonate. Finally, stir in the flour, loosening with a little milk if necessary. Tip the mixture onto a floured work surface and use your hands to bring together into a well-mixed ball of dough. Wrap in film and pop in the fridge for 30 minutes to firm up.

5 Heat the oven to 180C(160C fan), Gas 4. Line a couple of oven trays with baking parchment. Roll a piece of dough to a 2cm-sized ball, then place on the lined tray. Use the palm of your hand to flatten out the ball, to about 4cm in diameter. Repeat with the rest of the mixture – it might be that you have to do the biscuits in batches; keep the dough chilled if this is the case while a batch is in the oven. Bake for 20 minutes, then transfer to a cooling rack.

6 For the crystallized violets, spoon the caster sugar onto a small saucer or piece of baking parchment. Give the egg white a light whisk until starting to look frothy, then use a small paintbrush to coat a violet flower. Carefully sprinkle the sugar over the petals; try to completely cover them if possible. Repeat with the remaining flowers, then leave to dry in a light, airy spot for a minimum of an hour.

7 Spoon a 1½ tsp of curd onto the underside of a biscuit, then gently place another biscuit on top. Sprinkle a few crystallized violets over each biscuit when serving. The left-over curd will keep for about a month in the fridge after it has been opened.

Medlar jelly is great on a cheeseboard, or used as you would redcurrant jelly to sweeten a stock or gravy. This recipe works for quince and crab apple jellies too; quince will need a while longer simmering in the water to break down, but the juice-sugar ratios are the same.

Medlar jelly

1kg bletted medlars

granulated sugar

juice of 1 lemon

Kit:

jelly bag

sterilized jars

1 Roughly quarter the fruit and put into a saucepan. Cover with water, bring to the boil and simmer for a good half an hour or so until soft and pulpy. Tip everything into a jelly bag, then leave overnight to strain into a bowl.

2 Measure the juice and pour into a clean pan, along with 375g sugar for every 500ml of liquid. Squeeze in the lemon juice and bring to the boil.

3 Keep on the heat, stirring regularly until it has reached setting point. You'll know it's ready when a small blob cooled on a saucer wrinkles when you push your finger through it. Spoon into sterilized jars – this jelly should keep for at least a year if stored in a cool, dry place.

I'm fortunate enough to get a decent crop of Jerusalem artichokes from the garden each year. Not that this is in any way planned I might add – I'm convinced that I've dug them all up each winter, but a few tubers always seem to slip through the net and poke shoots up in spring. A single partridge is just about right for one person; they have a terrific gamey flavour which is well-matched by the sweet medlar sauce and nutty artichoke purée in this recipe.

Roast partridge, Jerusalem artichoke purée & medlar & juniper sauce

Serves 4

For the purée:

400g Jerusalem artichokes

1 medium-sized potato

splash of hot milk

knob of butter

For the partridges:

4 partridges

4 knobs of butter

For the sauce:

splash of Calvados

2tsp medlar jelly (see page 145)

250ml game or chicken stock

sprig of fresh thyme

6 juniper berries

1 Peel the artichokes and potato, then boil in salted water until soft. Drain and quickly transfer to a blender along with the hot milk and salt and pepper. Blitz to a smooth purée, and then pass through a sieve if any lumps remain. Check the seasoning and stir in the butter.

2 Preheat the oven to 200C(180C fan), Gas 6. Season the partridges, arrange in an oven and hob-proof dish and place a knob of butter on the breast of each bird. Roast for 20-25 minutes until golden and the juices run clear, then set aside on a plate to rest (upside down so that the partridge breasts are facing downwards).

3 Heat the roasting pan on the hob and de-glaze with a splash of Calvados. Stir in the medlar jelly, stock, thyme and juniper; bring to a quick bubble and reduce to a thick sauce. Pass through a sieve before serving but keep hold of the juniper berries; a couple always look good in the sauce when plating. Serve with crusty bread and winter salad leaves, such as radicchio and chicory.

An unusual dish; you're unlikely to find many recipes that feature whole bletted medlars but I urge you to give this one a try.

Custard-baked medlars with a crumble topping

Serves 4

100g plain flour

100g unsalted butter, grated

25g oats

25g flaked almonds, very lightly chopped

50g light muscovado sugar

For the custard:

100ml double cream

350ml whole milk

2 large egg yolks

35g caster sugar

1 tbsp cornflour

½ tsp good quality vanilla extract

8-12 bletted medlars, depending on size

zest of 1 orange

1 Heat the oven to 180C(160C fan), Gas 4. Use your fingertips to rub the flour and butter together until you have a breadcrumb-like consistency, then stir in the oats, almonds and sugar. Line a baking sheet with parchment, scatter over the crumble mix and bake for 15 minutes. Break the crumble up with a spoon, then bake for a further 10 minutes. Set aside to cool.

2 Make the custard. Warm the cream and milk in pan on a gentle heat, stirring intermittently until it's just below boiling point. In a separate bowl, whisk the egg yolks, sugar, cornflour and vanilla extract together until combined, then gradually whisk in the hot creamy milk. Pour the mixture back into the saucepan and stir on a low heat for 6-8 minutes until the custard has thickened (make sure that it never boils). Leave to cool for a few minutes, then pour into an oven-proof dish (approximately 20cm x 15cm in size). Glance over the medlars and trim off the spiney persistent sepals then nestle into the custard-filled dish. Grate over the orange zest and bake for 25 minutes. Sprinkle over the crumble pieces about 5 minutes from the end of the cooking time to give them a chance to warm through.

Orchard drinks

Orchard drinks

I'm a great fan of what you might term 'project cooking'. These are recipes that involve intermittent levels of hands-on involvement over a period of time; it's not about shirking effort as such, more a case of having several things on the go at once that fit in and around other things that I'm working on. A quick glance inside a covered bowl here, a gentle shake of a bottle there; one needs to set aside time at certain stages along the way, but for the most part things are ticking away nicely in your absence. One of the main areas of kitchen life that suits this ethos perfectly is home curing and smoking, the other is drinks making.

It often feels that the orchard gathers momentum towards one key event each year. I try to store as much fruit as I can, but the reality is that space can be an issue and many varieties of apple just don't keep. Gluts can quickly become overwhelming once a tree has established itself, especially if you don't want to waste any of your valuable crop. The answer is simple – a busy weekend in late autumn spent gathering and juicing apples.

Juicing can be a pretty hands-on affair depending of the extent of your kit. In Year One it took us about half a day of working flat-out with a tiny apple press to produce what felt like a meagre amount of juice. It was good fun, but squeezing litre after litre of liquid through a press roughly the size of a large baked bean tin left me a shadow of my former self, disheveled and covered in apple pulp. It's a much more civilized affair these days; the current press yields 5 litres of liquid every time that it's filled. I manage to set aside a few litres of juice to pasteurize, but for the most part it's used for cider. After the initial burst of activity juicing the apples, things settle down for a little while. It takes a couple of weeks or so for the cider to ferment, but this time can vary depending on the temperature, so it pays to keep an eye on proceedings.

The hardest part of the process is waiting for the cider to be ready to drink once it's been bottled. Damson gin and medlar brandy require a similar degree of patience and a steady resolve, but one can take comfort from the fact that with every day or week that a bottle lies unopened, the contents will be improving slowly inside.

Sakurayu is a cherry blossom infusion traditionally served at weddings and receptions in Japan. The expression 'Ocha wo nigosu' refers to green tea and translates as 'Make the tea cloudy', which is seen as symbolically inappropriate at the union of a couple. In contrast, Sakurayu is perfectly clear and represents a pure, uncloudy beginning to a marriage. It has a lightly salty, floral taste which is quite refreshing.

Sakurayu – salted cherry blossoms

bowl of freshly picked cherry
blossoms with stalks

sea salt

200ml Ume plum vinegar

1 Soak the flowers in water for a few minutes, then transfer to a sieve or colander to drip-dry. Scatter a layer of sea salt crystals across the bottom of a glass bowl, follow with a layer of blossoms and then repeat the process until all the flowers are covered in salt. Rest a small saucer on top to apply a bit of pressure and leave overnight.

2 Pick the flowers out of the salt and transfer to smaller glass bowl. Cover with plum vinegar, making sure that they are completely submerged. Leave to soak for three days.

3 Strain the blossoms, sprinkle with salt and air-dry on kitchen paper – make sure that they're sitting in a well-ventilated spot. If dried properly they'll keep in an air tight tin for months; just add a teaspoon of dried flowers to a cup and add boiling hot water.

There's no question that apple and blackcurrant are trusted bedfellows; it might seem unusual to use the leaves as a flavouring but it really works and the taste is distinct. The inclusion of elderflower makes this a perfect early summer drink; seasonal, refreshing and vibrant.

Apple, elderflower & blackcurrant leaf gin spritzer

For the cordial:

7 large elderflower heads

7 large blackcurrant leaves

1 unwaxed lemon, zest pared with a potato peeler and lemon cut into slices

1 litre water

25g citric acid

500g caster sugar

For the spritzer:

100ml elderflower and blackcurrant cordial

100ml gin

ice

750ml chilled soda water

250ml apple juice

apple slices

mint leaves

1 First, make the cordial. Place the flowers and leaves in a large bowl, along with the lemon slices and zest. Bring the water and sugar to the boil in a saucepan; let it cool for 5 minutes, then pour into the bowl. Stir in the citric acid, cover with a tea towel and set to one side for 24 hours.

2 Strain the cordial through muslin, then decant into sterilized bottles.

3 To make the spritzer, put a large handful of ice into the bottom of a jug and stir in the cordial, gin and mint leaves. Then add the chilled soda water, apple juice and apple slices.

My first foray into cider making started relatively small-scale, using a variety of apple sources and very basic kit. The apples were either: procured from trees in our neighbour's gardens (with permission I should add), foraged, or taken from a cider apple tree rather cannily planted by my brewing partner Leon in his mother's back garden twenty years ago. Sadly, the results weren't great first time round; the cider had a good apple flavour, but to be honest, it was a touch vinegary.

A couple of years' ago we befriended a local farmer who very kindly let us gather as many apples from his orchard as we could, in exchange for a percentage of the cider. This was more than a fair deal as far as I'm concerned; the apples make great cider, while the recipe has been fine-tuned over the years to produce a superb drink. I've kept things small-scale to start you off, but if you want to make a greater volume of cider simply keep the ratios the same and scale up the ingredients. A batch made in the autumn should be nearly ready to drink the following spring, but if you can hold off until summer it'll be all the better.

Cider

4.5 litres freshly squeezed apple juice

1 Campden tablet

malic acid

precipitated chalk

2tsp pectolase

dextrose (brewing sugar)

5g sachet brewing yeast

1tsp yeast nutrient

artificial sweetener

Kit:

a demijohn or food-grade brewing container

pH meter

hydrometer

500ml strong glass cider bottles, sterilized

bottle tops

bottle capper

1 It's important to be super-fastidious about hygiene when making cider; any rogue bacteria sneaking into your brew could cause it to spoil. Pour the apple juice into a sterilized demi-john or container, then crush and stir in the Campden tablet. This kills all of the natural yeasts in the juice – which may sound perverse, but having experienced the tiresome clear-up of an exploded bottle of home brew I personally favour a greater level of control and add my own brewing yeast.

2 Next, check the acidity of the juice. You're looking for a pH reading of between 3.6 and 4.2 pH – add malic acid if the pH reading is too low and precipitated chalk if the acidity is too high. Adjust gradually, stirring well and leaving for a good 10-15 minutes each time before re-testing. Once the acidity is right stir in the Pectolase; this enhances the flavour of the cider and ensures that your brew isn't cloudy.

3 Fermentable sugars in the juice are turned into alcohol when the brewing yeast is added; by using a hydrometer one can measure sugar levels and estimate the resultant strength of the brew. Most modern hydrometers will be marked with a predicted alcohol scale; we favour an ABV of around the 6.5% mark, which might seem quite strong, but it makes for a

cider that will keep for longer. If the sugar content is too low stir in dextrose. If it looks like your cider might clock in any higher than 8%, add water to bring the sugar level down. Test regularly until you're happy.

4 Stir in the brewing yeast and yeast nutrient. Leave the cider to ferment at a temperature of 15 - 22 degrees for 1 - 2 weeks; the juice will form a sort of sponge on the surface, which then sinks to the bottom when the cider is nearly ready. A test with the hydrometer will establish whether or not fermentation is still happening. By the end of the process all sugars will have been converted to alcohol.

5 Sweeten to taste with artificial sweetener. Purists may be aghast at this inclusion, but from past experience I've had batches that have turned out way too sharp and prefer not to run the gauntlet. Artificial sweetener won't ferment and the taste of the cider is in no way compromized.

6 Siphon the cider into sterilized, bottles. Add ½ a teaspoon of caster sugar into each bottle before capping; this stirs up a mini-ferment in the sealed bottle, and gives it a bit of sparkle when poured. Your cider will be flat if you skip this step, which some people like but isn't my personal preference.

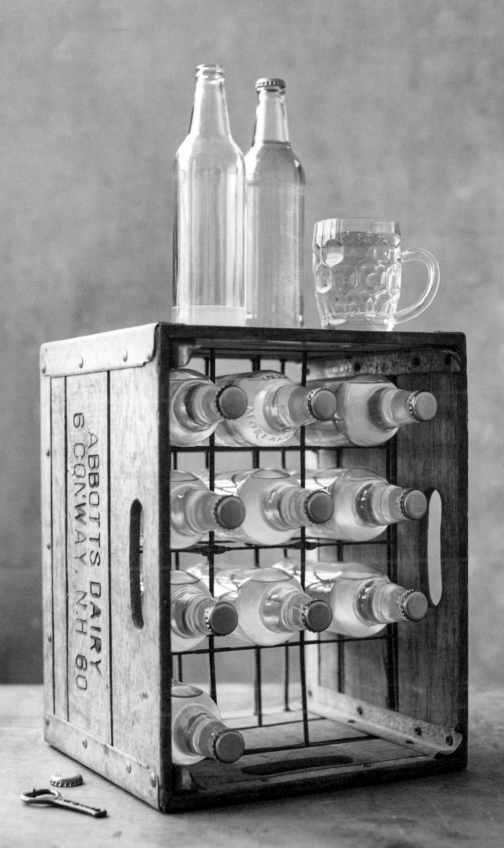

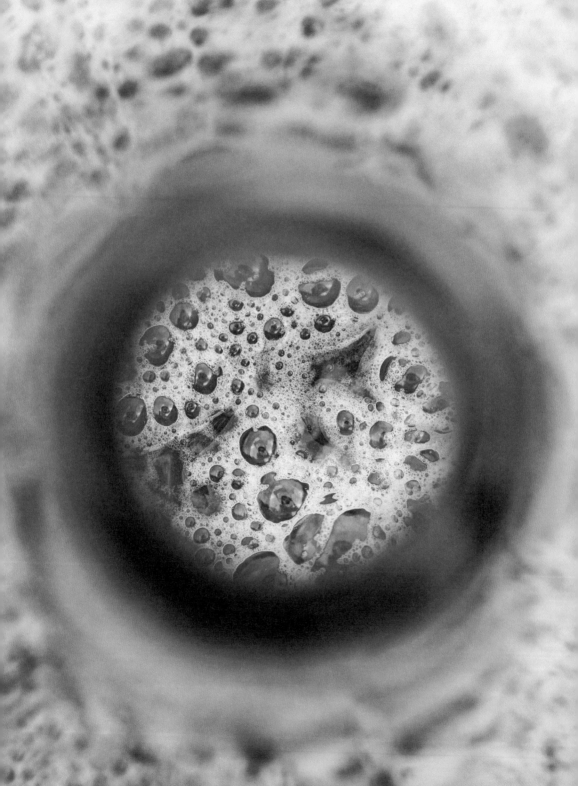

You might guffaw at the inclusion of an apple juice recipe in this book; and yes – the basic principle of juicing a few apples barely needs explaining. How long this juice keeps for though is another matter. Un-pasteurized apple juice will last for 2 to 3 days before it starts to ferment, but take a little time to pasteurize when bottling and many of the natural enzymes that kick-start fermentation are killed. Pasteurized apple juice can last for up to 2 years, plus it's easy to do. As ever, super-snazzy specialist equipment is available to buy, but you really only need a large, deep pan, glass bottles with screw top lids and a thermometer. Ascorbic acid (vitamin C) prevents the juice from going brown; this process works when bottling any fresh fruit juice.

Apple juice

5 litres of freshly pressed apple juice

1tsp (heaped) ascorbic acid

1 Stir the ascorbic acid into the apple juice, then pour into sterilized 1-litre glass bottles, leaving a 5cm gap at the top of each (the juice expands when heated, plus the level rises further when the thermometer sits in the bottle). Sit in a large pan on the hob, then pour water around the bottles, bringing the level up so that the juice is two-thirds covered. Pop a long brewing thermometer into one of the bottles, then heat the water in the pan until the juice in the bottles reaches 75 degrees. Remove the bottles from the water bath and cap immediately; once the lids are tightly screwed on put the bottles onto their sides (this helps to sterilize the inside of the caps). Store in a cool place out of the sun.

I often make this at the end of summer, when there's the faintest curl of autumn in the tips of the leaves and a jug of classic Pimm's just doesn't feel quite appropriate. You could use pear juice in place of apple; there's also nothing to stop you adding a few extra fruits and botanicals. Quartered plums, orange slices, pomegranate seeds, star anise and a vanilla pod would be worthy additions.

Orchard punch

ice

500ml Pimm's

300ml Calvados

1.5 litres apple Juice

2 eating apples, thinly sliced

2 sweet pears, thinly sliced

2 Cinnamon sticks

I Put a good handful of ice in the bottom of a large bowl and add the Pimm's and Calvados. Top up with apple juice and stir through with the sliced fruit and cinnamon sticks.

A glass of chilled fizz is a wonderful thing in its own right, but sometimes I'm after a bit more – the orchard offers up plenty of opportunities to take a glass of bubbles up to the next level.

5 Orchard fizz recipes

Medlar brandy champagne cocktail

Drop a sugar cube into the bottom of a champagne flute. Carefully shake in 4 or 5 drops of Angostura bitters, then almost cover the sugar cube with medlar brandy. Top up with champagne.

Cherry, kirsch & amaretto fizz

Soak a handful of de-stoned and halved cherries in a generous splash of kirsch, then leave to macerate (do this a few hours before the cocktail hour chimes – give the cherries a stir every once in a while). Pour 1cm amaretto into a champagne flute, then drop 4 of the cherry halves into the glass. Top up with champagne.

Membrini

Mash 2 sugar cube-sized chunks of membrillo and juice of 1 clementine together into a smooth paste, then pour into the bottom of a champagne flute. Top up with champagne.

Damson Royale

Pour 1cm damson gin into the bottom of a champagne flute, then top up with champagne. Finish with a blackberry.

Pear & ginger fizz

I use the syrup from a jar of stem ginger when I make this cocktail, although you can also buy bottles of ginger syrup online. Pour 1cm ginger syrup into the bottom of a champagne flute. Make up to about 3cm with pear juice; top the glass up with champagne, give it a gentle stir and finish with a few slices of thinly sliced fresh pear.

Perfect fare if you're feeling a bit fragile from the night before.
I find that adding apple juice brings an extra hint of sweetness
that works perfectly with the heat of tobasco and horseradish.
Leave out the tequila to make this a virgin apple Maria.

Bloody apple Maria

Makes I drink

5 ice cubes

25ml Tequila (this is a single measure; double-up if it's been a tough week)

juice of ½ a lime

I tsp freshly grated horseradish

4 dashes of Worcestershire sauce

6 dashes of Tabasco (I like my Bloody Maria spicy)

pinch of celery salt

good grind of black pepper

200ml tomato juice

50ml apple juice

I celery stick

few slices of fresh apple, to serve

I Tip the ice into a glass and pour in the tequila. Add the lime juice, horseradish, Worcestershire sauce, tabasco, celery salt, pepper and half of the tomato and apple juice and give it a good stir with a spoon. Pour in the remaining juices, mix well again and serve with a celery stick and slices of fresh apple.

When I made my first bottle of damson gin about ten years ago, I was told to use the cheapest gin that I could find, as it had no bearing on the quality of the finished product. While it's true that inexpensive gin does make a perfectly satisfactory bottle to drink, if you are able to splash out on better quality gin I assure you that it really does translate into a deeper, more complex flavour. Whether it's added to a stock reduction, lightly sweetening a tagine or simply drizzled over ice cream for a quick dessert, a bottle of damson gin is a valuable addition to the kitchen (as well as the drinks cupboard, of course). The same ratios apply when making medlar brandy; simply replace the gin with brandy and the damsons with chopped medlars.

Damson gin

75cl gin

300g granulated sugar

damsons

Equipment:

large glass jar or bottle

1 Pour the gin into your jar or bottle, then stir in the sugar. Top up to the gin level with damsons; piercing the skin of each sends inky plumes darting through the gin – a pin or fork will do the trick. Gently agitate the bottle daily for the first 7 days and weekly thereafter.

2 After two months strain the liquid and re-bottle; leave for at least two months before sampling. Don't throw the macerated damsons away, they can be de-stoned and used in other recipes.

The kids and I go wassailing every January without fail; it's a fine evening of tradition, theatre and a hearty dose of paganism. A torch-lit procession starts at the far-end of the village and makes its way towards the orchard; as we approach, pots and pans are banged and rattled to scare away evil spirits and ensure a good harvest in the autumn. Toast soaked in wassail is hung on an apple tree as a gift to the spirits; wassail is sipped and there is singing and dancing.

Cider & damson gin wassail

150g crab apples or 6 small eating apples

2 tbsp brown sugar

1.5 litres cider

250ml damson gin

200g caster sugar

1 orange, sliced

thumb-sized piece of root ginger, thinly sliced

2 cinnamon sticks

2 star anise

6 allspice berries

4 cloves

¼ of a nutmeg, freshly grated

To serve:

4 slices of white toast, cut into triangles

1 Heat the oven to 180C(160C fan), Gas 4. Toss the apples in the brown sugar and transfer to an oven-proof dish; roast for 20 minutes until the apples have partly softened and the skins are starting to split. Set aside to cool.

2 Stir the cider, damson gin, apples, caster sugar, orange, ginger and spices together in a large pan, then bring to a simmer on a hob or fire. Serve in mugs or handled glasses with toast to dip into the wassail.

A good slosh of damson gin is a worthy addition to a mug of rich, hot chocolate; the sweet, plummy notes of damson and a touch of bitterness from dark chocolate make for an indulgent treat.

Damson gin hot chocolate

Serves 1

100g dark chocolate

600ml whole milk

150ml double cream

50ml damson gin

1 Chop the chocolate, then add to a saucepan with the milk and cream. Bring to a slow boil, whisking regularly to help dissolve any rogue lumps of chocolate.

2 Stir in the damson gin just before serving.

Smoked

Smoked

I love these early autumn days. There's a familiar note in the air; crisp mornings warmed gently by a thin sun, scented with an earthy perfume of wood, wet leaves and smoke. It's a bit early to think about pruning the fruit trees in the orchard, but I have a few bundles of year-old seasoned apple, pear, plum and cherry wood that are ready to use for smoking.

The best time to prune a fruit tree varies depending on type; I always set aside some twigs and small branches when doing so – they'll need to sit in a dry spot for at least a month or two before they are ready to use, after which a small wood chipper is your best bet for breaking them down. Chippers can be quite expensive though; I've used a pencil sharpener in the past – often you don't need many shavings for small-scale hot smoking and it actually works a treat. Apple, cherry and plum wood chips are readily available online if you don't have access to fruit tree cuttings.

Hot smoking

Hot smoking is essentially an all year-round affair, yet there is something about the complex, smoky notes imparted by the process that lend themselves towards produce more associated with the autumn and winter months. You can use a wok for hot smoking; simply line the bottom of the pan with kitchen foil, scatter over a handful of wood chips and heat on a barbecue or hob. Place a large round wire rack inside, ensuring that it sits a good 4-6cm above the foil, but not flush with the rim. Add your meat, fish or fruit, then cover with more foil – make sure to uncover the wok outside after cooking as plenty of smoke will escape. (See page 200.)

Cold smoking

An altogether more complex endeavour, yet just as rewarding and in some ways a lot more creative. Smoke is created in a primary chamber; this smoke then passes through to a second, often larger chamber containing the food, having cooled in the process. Due to the absence of direct heat, cold smoking is an altogether lengthier process than hot smoking; it is also a predominantly outdoor-based, winter pursuit. A consistent ambient temperature of less than 3 degrees Celsius is essential inside the second chamber and is an important health and safety consideration; one might be cold smoking a side of bacon for over 12 hours, so holding out for a cold snap is a must.

*This will be the best bacon sandwich that you've ever eaten.
I favour a light 3-day cure for my bacon, but if you prefer a saltier
streaky that will keep for longer, increase the sugar and salt to
500g and cure for 5-6 days. Make sure that you use the best
quality, organic free-range pork that you can get your hands on.*

Cold-smoked streaky bacon

For the cure:

300g fine salt

300g granulated sugar

2tsp black peppercorns, freshly
ground

2kg pork belly, skin removed

To smoke:

apple, pear, plum or cherry wood
chips

Kit:

cold smoker

1 Mix the cure ingredients together. Scatter a handful (roughly 100g) of cure across the bottom of a clean, food box or tray and place the pork belly on top. Sprinkle another 100g of cure on top and give the meat a good rub all over. Cover with a tea towel and leave in the fridge for 24 hours – keep the remaining cure in a sealed container. The next day, drain off and discard any liquid from the container and repeat the process for 2 more days with the same amount of cure. The meat should feel notably firmer the longer it cures.

2 Rinse the meat with cold water and pat dry with kitchen paper. Remove a shelf from the middle of the fridge and wedge a length of dowel into the shelf grooves on either side; put a meat hook through the bacon and hang it off the dowel, ensuring good airflow all round. Leave to dry in the fridge for 24 hours.

3 Cold-smoking time is dependent on the efficiency of your smoker. Mine is a homemade affair; an oak smoking-chamber served by a small incinerator, connected by a length of metal tubing. Hot coals are placed in the bottom of the incinerator, after which a handful of damp wood chips are sprinkled on top. These chips need to be topped up as-and-when. Managing the airflow through the incinerator keeps things ticking along nicely; too much air and the chips will catch fire, too little and the embers will go out. My bacon takes about 5 hours, but yours could take up to 12. Getting a feel for your smoker is part of the fun of the process; it's a bit of effort initially but the hands-on time is minimal once you're up and smoking.

There's something a bit special about smoking a side of halibut, a fish rightly considered by many as the king of the flatfish. I love the colours in this starter; the redcurrants bring little pops of sharpness, while there's plenty of fresh crunch in there from the radishes and radicchio leaves.

Smoked halibut with radicchio, radish & redcurrant

Serves 4 as a starter

To cure the halibut:

750g fresh halibut fillet

75g fine sea salt

75g light brown sugar

To smoke:

apple, pear, plum or cherry wood chips

For the salad:

200g smoked halibut

2 small radicchio

1 small watermelon radish, thinly sliced

16 large breakfast radishes, thinly sliced

30g redcurrants

small handful of wasabi shoots

For the dressing:

3tbsp olive oil

2tbsp white wine vinegar

Kit:

cold smoker

1 Pat the halibut dry with kitchen paper and lay skin-side down on a large baking tray. Mix the salt and sugar together, then spread the cure evenly over the flesh. Wrap the tray in cling film and leave in the fridge for a minimum of 8 hours, 3 days maximum (the length of the cure will affect the saltiness of the fish).

2 Rinse the cure off the halibut with cold water, then pat dry with kitchen paper. The fish needs to be completely dry before smoking, so leave it unwrapped on a tray in a well-ventilated fridge for 24 hours.

3 Cold smoke the halibut. Duration will depend on the efficiency of your smoker; a piece of fish this size takes 4 - 6 hours in my smoker. To serve, slice thinly, cutting away from the widest end of the fillet (the head end).

4 Plate up the smoked halibut with the salad ingredients, then drizzle over with dressing and season just before serving.

This isn't really one for date night – there's a whole bulb of garlic in there but it tastes oh so much better for it. The idea of incorporating thin layers of smoked fish into a layered, potato gratin is based around Laxpudding – a classic Swedish recipe. I'm using smoked halibut here instead of salmon for an extra level of decadence. This is proper winter fare, best served with a bitter-leaf salad and a glass of beer.

Smoked halibut & roasted garlic & celeriac dauphinoise

Serves 4

1 garlic bulb

100ml milk

150ml double cream

1 bay leaf

500g waxy potato

250g celeriac

200g smoked halibut, thinly sliced (see page 184)

a small bunch of fresh thyme

100g Gruyere cheese

1 Heat the oven to 180C(160C fan), Gas 4. Roast the bulb whole on a baking tray for 25 minutes until golden brown and soft. Leave it to cool for 10 minutes, then remove the softened garlic pulp.

2 Blitz the garlic and milk in a food processor, then add to a saucepan with the cream and bay leaf. Season and bring to a gentle simmer – careful not to let it erupt into a fast boil.

3 Peel the potato and celeriac and using a mandolin, thinly slice. Then in an oven proof dish, create alternating layers of potato, celeriac and halibut, scattering thyme leaves intermittently. End with a layer of potato on top, giving you 7 layers in total. Remove the bay leaf from the cream and pour the mixture over the layers. Top with grated Gruyere and cover with kitchen foil. Bake for 40 minutes, then remove the foil and cook for a further 35-40 minutes, until the cheese is golden and a sharp knife slips easily through the layers.

If you're firing up the cold smoker for a good half-day smoking session, it makes perfect sense to get a few things ready to go in the chamber at once to maximize output. Sliding a wedge of cheese onto the top shelf above any hanging meat or fish takes zero prep and tastes out of this world. Choose a good mature Cheddar to smoke; these scones will keep for a day or two in a tin and are great served with smoked salmon and a few thin slices of cucumber.

Cheddar, dill & apple scones with caramelized cider onion chutney

Makes 8 scones

For the chutney:

500g white onions

2 bay leaves

70cl bottle of cider

100g light muscovado sugar

75ml cider vinegar

1tsp chilli flakes

For the scones:

200g self-raising flour

½tsp baking powder

1tsp salt

few grinds of black pepper

50g butter, chopped into small cubes

1 eating apple

100g grated smoked mature cheddar, plus a bit extra to sprinkle on top

small bunch of dill fronds, roughly chopped

125-150ml milk

To serve:

slices of Cheddar

1 For the chutney cut the onions in half, peel, slice and season. Warm a splash of oil in a heavy bottomed pan on a medium heat; then add the onions and bay. Stir gently while the onions start to soften in the pan, then begin to pour in the cider – a small amount at a time. Stir intermittently as the liquid absorbs into the onions; continue the process until any liquid has gone from the pan. Turn the heat down to low and continue to stir, more frequently now that the cider has gone, so that the onions don't catch. You're after soft, caramelized onions with a toffee-like colour, all in all the process might take as long as 90 minutes, but patience is rewarded.

2 Stir in the sugar, vinegar and chilli flakes, then keep on a low bubble for 30-45 minutes. Let it cool for a bit and then spoon into sterilised jars.

3 For the scones: preheat the oven to 220C(200C fan), Gas 7. Sieve the flour and baking powder into a large mixing bowl, stir in the salt and pepper, then add the butter. Use your fingertips to work the flour and butter together, until you have a breadcrumb-like consistency. Peel, core and chop the apple and mix with the Cheddar and dill, then slowly pour in the milk to form a dough (make sure that it's not too sticky).

4 Shape the dough into a round on a floured surface (roughly 2cm deep), then use a knife to cut it into 8 wedges. Place on a parchment flour-dusted baking sheet, sprinkle some spare cheddar on top and bake for 15 minutes. Serve warm with thick slices of mature Cheddar and dollops of onion chutney.

I know I know – schlepping out to the woods on a frosty March morning to drill a hole in the trunk of a tree might not be everyone's cup of tea, but birch syrup is hard to come by; it's expensive and it's actually quite fun making it yourself. If I'm out of birch syrup I'll use maple syrup which is easily as good; this hot-smoked salmon has just the right balance of smoky, salty and sweet, and if you wrap it in clingfilm it will keep in the fridge for a good couple of weeks.

Birch-glazed hot-smoked salmon

For the silver birch syrup:

2 litres fresh silver birch sap

4 tbsp granulated sugar

To cure the salmon:

1 kg side of salmon

250g salt

250g dark brown sugar

To smoke:

apple wood chips

100ml birch or maple syrup

Kit:

hot smoker

1 To collect the syrup: find a good sturdy birch, well off the beaten track. At a smooth point on the trunk about 60cm from the ground, drill a hole approximately 4cm deep at an upward angle, then insert a thin piece of tubing into the hole as sap starts to trickle out. A large bottle or demijohn, neck wedged over the tube, will collect the sap. This is by no means a sprightly endeavour, so come back the next morning to collect the liquid. Wedge a piece of dowel into the hole to stop the flow, then cover with a bit of clay to create an extra seal.

2 Bring the birch sap to the boil, stir in the sugar and reduce to approximately a twentieth of its original volume; this gets rid of most of the water and the sugary birch flavour intensifies – you're looking for the syrup to have a light amber colour. Set aside to cool.

3 To cure the salmon, rinse it with cold water and pat dry with kitchen paper – remove any bones sticking out with a pair of tweezers. Scatter a handful of cure across the bottom of a food container, then lay the salmon on top (skin-side down). Sprinkle over the remaining cure, cover with a kitchen towel and refrigerate for 8 hours. Rinse off the cure and pat dry; the salmon needs to air-dry, so sit it skin-side down on a tray in the fridge for a minimum of 4 hours – overnight if possible.

4 Brush the salmon with birch syrup and place skin-side-down in your hot smoker. Smoke for 35 minutes, brushing with syrup intermittently.

*I'll make this at the end of a long day when I'm after something
quick, vibrant and colourful and the first of the season's apples are
ready to be picked. Peppery nasturtiums are my go-to salad leaf in
the summer months; they are really easy to grow and the flowers
are also edible.*

Applewood hot-smoked salmon with chicory, apple & honey lemon dressing

Serves 4

For the salad:

4 small chicory heads

2 sweet eating apples

4 radishes

½ red onion

400g birch glazed hot-smoked
salmon (see page 193)

nasturtium leaves (use watercress
if you can't find them)

chives

For the dressing:

4tbsp olive oil

2tsp honey

juice of ½ a lemon

salt and pepper

1 Slice the chicory heads in half lengthways. Brush with a little oil then griddle or barbecue flat-side down, just enough to char and soften the chicory.

2 Use a mandolin slicer to thinly slice the apple, radish and onion. There's no need to core the apple in this instance; the slices should be paper-thin – any very slight bitter notes are usurped by the chicory. Do remove the pips though.

3 Mix the dressing ingredients together. Plate up the chicory, apple, radish and onion, then flake over the hot-smoked salmon. Scatter with nasturtium leaves and chopped chives, then spoon over the dressing.

*A bit of retrospective karma-alignment; my feathered chums
decimated the cherry crop again this year.*

Smoked pigeons on horseback

**Serves 4 as a light lunch
or starter.**

60g cherries

2tbsp damson gin

8 pigeon breasts

8 strips of pancetta

sprig of rosemary

To smoke:

cherry wood chips

To serve:

sourdough bread

watercress

1 Stone the cherries and slice into quarters. Pop into a small bowl, stir in the damson gin and leave overnight to macerate (or for a decent few hours at least – it's a good idea to give them a stir once in a while if you can).

2 Season the pigeon breasts well with sea salt and freshly cracked black pepper; let them sit for about 10 minutes then hot smoke over cherry wood chips for 4-5 minutes. Remove from the heat and set aside to until the meat is cool enough to handle.

3 Put the pigeon breasts face-down on a board; fat, curved side facing your knife blade. Carefully slice a pocket lengthways into each breast; I tend to cut just over half way along. Push 3 or 4 cherry quarters into each breast (depending on breast size), close the flap and then carefully wrap with pancetta.

4 Heat a splash of oil in a frying pan with the rosemary. Place the wrapped breasts into the hot oil, then fry for 1 minute before turning and cooking for a further minute on the other side. Leave to rest for 5 minutes before serving. Serve on slices of sourdough bread with some watercress.

Crayfish respond exceptionally well to smoking; the sharpness of blood orange, saltiness of samphire and a kick of iron from cavolo nero lift this simple salad into something rather noteworthy. The smoked crayfish would also be great spooned into chicory leaves to serve as a canâpé, with a grating of fresh horseradish, lemon juice and herbs from the garden.

Hot-smoked crayfish with samphire, blood orange & cavelo nero

Serves 4 as a starter

For the smoked crayfish:

24 live crayfish, kept in fresh changes of water for about 2 days (change the water every couple of hours to keep it oxygenated)

apple, pear, cherry or plum wood chips

For the salad:

100g cavolo nero, thick ribs removed

75g samphire

2 large blood oranges, peeled and sliced

1 small kohlrabi, sliced with a mandolin

For the dressing:

3tbsp olive oil

2tbsp blood orange juice

salt and pepper

To serve:

garlic chive shoots

Kit:

hot smoker

1 A couple of hours before you plan to cook and smoke the crayfish, cover a deep freezer tray with ice, arrange the crayfish on top and return to the freezer. This slowly renders the crayfish unconscious, which is ultimately a more humane way of preparing them before cooking. Bring a large pan of salted water to the boil, quickly tip the crayfish in and pop the lid on. Boil for 3 minutes, then drain and leave to cool until comfortable to pick up.

2 Hot smoke the crayfish for 15-20 minutes, then leave to cool. Remove the tail meat; keeping them in the fresh water should have purged them but check the tail for a little black line just in case and remove it.

3 Mix the dressing ingredients together. Steam the cavolo nero and samphire for 3-4 minutes; once cooled toss together with the crayfish, blood orange and kohlrabi. Drizzle with the dressing and sprinkle over garlic chive shoots just before serving.

The idea of hot-smoking mussels is partly inspired by my fondness for éclade de moules; a French recipe that involves cooking fresh mussels with burning pine needles. There seems to be a certain affinity between mussels and smoke – fruit wood is particularly good in this instance.

Hot-smoked mussels with wasabi mayonnaise

Serves 2

For the wasabi mayo:

1 egg yolk, fresher the better

150ml rapeseed oil

squeeze of lemon juice

2tsp wasabi paste, or to taste if you like it hotter/milder

For the mussels:

1kg mussels, in shells

2 shallots, peeled and thickly sliced

2 garlic cloves, quartered

a wine glass of cider

To smoke:

apple, pear, cherry or plum wood chips

Kit:

hot smoker

1 For the wasabi mayo: put the egg yolk into a bowl and start whisk in the oil, adding a little at a time and making sure that it is thoroughly whisked in before you add more. The mixture will start to thicken; once you've added about half of the oil squeeze in the lemon juice which will thin the mixture out a little. Slowly whisk in the remaining oil, then stir in the wasabi paste and a pinch of salt.

2 Tip the mussels into a large bowl of water. Discard any that are open or have broken shells, then pull the little threads (or beards, as they are known) off. Use a knife to chip off any barnacles, then give the mussels a quick rinse with cold water.

3 Heat a splash of olive oil in a saucepan, then stir in the shallots and garlic. Soften on a low heat for a couple of minutes, then pour in the cider. Bring the heat up; when the cider is starting to bubble, tip the mussels in and place the lid on the pan. Give it a shake, then cook for 5-7 minutes. Shake the pan occasionally during this time – kill the heat when all the mussels have opened. Drain the mussels, picking out any pieces of garlic or shallot that have found their way inside the mussel shells.

4 Hot smoke the mussels in their shells for 10-15 minutes, then serve with the wasabi mayonnaise.

Many stone fruits respond well to smoke. I've had good results in the past with peaches and apricots, but one mustn't forget cherries. A really sweet cherry is key; I use scotch bonnet chillis in this sauce because they pack a punch and have fruitiness as well as heat that works well with the cherry and tomato. Smoked cherries can also be used to make a great digestif; simply mix 150g of caster sugar with 350ml bourbon, tip into a large jar and top up to the rim with smoked cherries that have been pierced with a fork. Shake every now and again – it'll be ready by Christmas...

Hot–smoked cherry & chilli sauce

200g cherries

3 medium tomatoes, de-seeded and chopped

2 Scotch bonnet chillis, de-seeded

2 shallots, finely chopped

2 cloves garlic, finely chopped

1 tbsp light muscovado sugar

150ml cider vinegar

100ml cherry juice

To smoke:

apple, pear, cherry or plum wood chips

Kit:

hot smoker

1 Cut a piece of kitchen foil that sits snugly inside your hot smoker. Pierce all over with a cocktail stick, then evenly space the cherries on top. Hot smoke for 10-15 minutes, then set aside to cool.

2 De-stone and chop the cherries, warm a splash of oil in a saucepan then stir in the cherries, tomatoes, chilli, shallots and garlic. Simmer on a medium heat for 10 minutes, stirring regularly.

3 Add the sugar, cider vinegar and cherry juice, along with a good pinch of sea salt. Bring to a bubble then simmer for another 10-15 minutes; remove from the heat and leave to cool for a short while.

4 Blitz the sauce in a food processor, then pass the blended mix through a sieve so that you have a smooth sauce. Check the seasoning – add a little more salt if needed. Pour into sterilized bottles; the sauce will keep for 6 months unopened.

Index

Acknowledgements

A great number of stylists and art directors have visited the studio in the time that I have been working on this book. Thanks for your continued advice, support and (perhaps most importantly) tolerance; especially when I whip out a work-in-progress dish for you to sample at 8:45am, when all you really want is a hot cup of coffee.

Thanks to Mum, Dad, Jenny, Ian, Carla, Bettina, Alex, Damien, Ross and John - the Ovenden and Roberts families, for your love and guidance over the years. I won't mention the furtive childhood scrumping trips if you don't.

It's been a pleasure to work with Catharine and Simonne at Clearview; I couldn't have wished for more assured and creative publishers. Thanks Lucy for your beautiful design, and to Suzannah for a discerning eye and sympathetic treatment of my words.

This book is for Victoria, the apple of my eye and little pips Amélie, Rafferty & Oscar.